Le Boom du Jour

Written & Illustrated
by B. K. Hixson

Le Boom du Jour

Copyright © 2002
First Printing • November 2002
B. K. Hixson

Published by Loose in the Lab, Inc.
9462 South 560 West
Sandy, Utah 84070

www.looseinthelab.com

Library of Congress Cataloging-in-Publication Data
Information Available Upon Request

Printed in the United States of America
Le Boom! Ooh la la!

Dedication

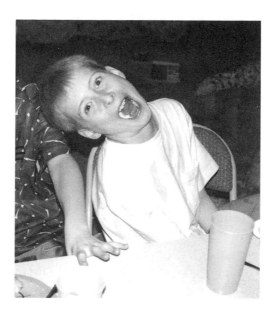

Dakota James Fagerbaake Hanson

What better book than "The Boom of the Day" to dedicate to an aspiring anarchist. It runs deep in your blood, as your grandpa would be happy to tell you, and it's one of those things that you either love or simply don't understand.

Here's to many happy hours mixing concoctions, dangling atoms from your fingertips, and creating new inventions to drip on the dog and chase your mom around the house with as they ooze up out of flasks. Wear your goggles, do what your mom tells you and be sure to send me photos of your escapades.

Hugs!

♡ Uncle Bryce

Acknowledgments

Getting a book out for public consumption is far from a one-man job. There are lots of thank-yous to be doodled out and at the risk of leaving someone out, we attempt to do that on this page. In terms of my chemistry education, at the top of the list is Mr. Ed Goffard, my fifth-grade teacher at Shaver Elementary School in Portland, Oregon. He introduced us to the world of crystals, solutions, precipitation reactions, and all of the wonderful treasures that could spring forth from a beaker. Next in line would be my buddy and colleague, Jerry "Wes" Westfall, for whom chemistry is not a study or discipline but rather an opportunity to live on the edge and push the envelope of social behavior to its acceptable limits. May your supply of oxidizers never run low.

As for my educational outlook, the hands-on perspective, and the use of humor in the classroom, Dr. Fox, my senior professor at Oregon State University, gets the credit for shaping my educational philosophy while simultaneously recognizing that even at the collegiate level we were on to something a little different. He did his very best to encourage, nurture, and support me while I was getting basketloads of opposition for being willing to swim upstream. There were also several colleagues who helped to channel my enthusiasm during those early, formative years of teaching: Dick Bishop, Dick Hinton, Dee Strange, Connie Ridgway, and Linda Zimmermann. Thanks for your patience, friendship, and support.

Next up are all the folks who get to do the dirty work that makes the final publication look so polished but very rarely get the credit they deserve. Our resident graphics guru, Kris Barton, gets a nod for scanning and cleaning the artwork you find on these pages, as well as putting together the graphics that make up the cover. A warm Yankee yahoo to Eve Laubner, our editor, who passes her comments on so that Kathleen Hixson and Eve Laubner (once again) can take turns simultaneously proofreading the text while mocking my writing skills.

Once we have a finished product, it is placed in the capable hands of Gary Facente, Louisa Walker, Tracy St. Pierre, Jay Brochu, and the Delta Education gang so they can market and ship the books, collect the money, and send us a couple of nickels. It's a short thank-you for several very important jobs.

Mom and Dad, as always, get the end credits. Thanks for the education, encouragement, and love. And for Kathy and the kids—Porter, Shelby, Courtney, and Aubrey—hugs and kisses.

Repro Rights

There is very little about this book that is truly formal, but at the insistence of our wise and esteemed counsel, let us declare: *No part of this book may be reproduced or utilized in any form or by any means, electronic or mechanical, including photocopying, recording, or by any information storage and retrieval system, without permission in writing from the publisher.* That would be us.

More Legal Stuff

Official disclaimer for you aspiring scientists and lab groupies. This is a hands-on science book. By the very intent of the design, you will be directed to use common, nontoxic, household items in a safe and responsible manner to avoid injury to yourself and others who are present while you are pursuing your quest for knowledge and enlightenment in the world of chemistry. Just make sure that you have a fire blanket handy and a wall-mounted video camera to corroborate your story.

If, for some reason, perhaps even beyond your own control, you have an affinity for disaster, we wish you well. *But we in no way take any responsibility for any injury that is incurred to any person using the information provided in this book or for any damage to personal property or effects that are directly or indirectly a result of the suggested activities contained herein.* Translation: You're on your own, despite the fact that many have preceded you in the lab. Take heed from our friend Johnny, who was a chemist, but is a chemist no more. For what he thought was H_2O was H_2SO_4.

Less Formal Legal Stuff

If you happen to be a home schooler or a very enthusiastic school teacher, please feel free to make copies of this book for your classroom or personal family use—one copy per student, up to 35 students. If you would like to use an experiment from this book for a presentation to your faculty or school district, we would be happy to oblige. Just give us a whistle and we will send you a release for the particular lab activity you wish to use. Please contact us at the address below. Thanks.

Special Requests
Loose in the Lab, Inc.
9462 South 560 West
Sandy, Utah 84070

Table of Contents

The National Content Standards (Grades 5-8)

  1. *A substance has characteristic properties, such as density, a boiling point, and solubility, all of which are independent of the amount of the sample. A mixture of substances often can be separated into the original substances using one or more of the characteristic properties.*

  2. *Substances react chemically in characteristic ways with other substances to form new substances (compounds) with different characteristic properties. In chemical reactions, the total mass is conserved. Substances often are placed in categories or groups if they react in similar ways; metals is an example of such a group.*

  3. *Chemical elements do not break down during normal laboratory reactions involving such treatments as heating, exposure to electric current, or reaction with acids. There are more than 100 known elements that combine in a multitude of ways to produce compounds, which account for the living and nonliving substances that we encounter.*

The 8 Big Ideas About Chemistry & Corresponding Labs

  1. Each kind of matter has a unique set of properties that allows the chemist to identify that matter. These properties include solubility, density, magnetism, flame test color, and melting point, which are all independent of the size of the sample.

2. Matter can exist in three different states: solid, liquid, or gas. Matter changes state when the temperature goes up or down. If matter changes state directly from solid to gas or from gas to solid, it is said to be undergoing the process of sublimation. Carbon dioxide is an excellent example of a compound that sublimates at room temperature.

3. Some chemicals release heat when they react with other compounds. These reactions are called exothermic reactions. Other chemicals absorb heat when they react with certain chemicals. These reactions are called endothermic reactions.

4. Liquids that allow an electric current to pass through them are called conductors. Electricity can be used to separate compounds into elements, attach compounds to one another, and produce changes in pH. Metals can also be used to generate the flow of electricity in the presence of electrical conductors.

Even More Contents

5. Compounds and elements can combine or bond with one another in groups of two or more. When this happens, a new compound is formed that has its own, unique set of characteristics and can be identified by a change of state, change of color, odor produced, light produced, or heat gain or loss.

6. The number of free ions in a solution is measured on a scale from 1 to 14, called the pH scale. A solution that tests at 7 is considered neutral, a solution below 7 is acidic, and a solution above 7 is basic. Specially prepared papers have been created to identify acids, bases, and degrees of pH.

7. Short, stumpity groups of molecules (called mers) can combine to form very long chains of molecules (called polymers). These molecules are characterized by their gooey, sticky ability to stretch and form long, elastic compounds that ooze and drip all over the place.

8. Some chemicals react with air and oxidize rapidly to produce large amounts of heat, light, and quite often, sound. We saved them for the end of the book because they are definitely the most fun but also require the most attention to safety.

Who Are You ? And ...

First of all, we may have an emergency at hand and we'll both want to cut to the chase and get the patient into the cardiac unit if necessary. So, before we go too much further, **define yourself**. Please check one and only one choice listed below and then immediately follow the directions that follow *in italics*. Thank you in advance for your cooperation.

I am holding this book because …

_____ **A. I am a responsible, but panicked, parent.** My son/daughter/triplets (circle one) just informed me that his/her/their science fair project is due tomorrow. This is the only therapy I could afford on such short notice. This means that, if I were not holding this book, my hands would be encircling the soon-to-be-worm-bait's neck.

Directions: Can't say this is the first or the last time we heard that one. Hang in there, we can do this.

1. Quickly read the table of contents with the worm bait. The Big Ideas define what each section is about. Obviously, the kid is not passionate about science or you would not be in this situation. See if you can find an idea that causes some portion of an eyelid or facial muscle to twitch.

If that does not work, we recommend narrowing the list to the following labs because they are fast, use materials that can be acquired with limited notice, and the intrinsic level of interest is generally quite high.

How to Use This Book

2. Take the materials list from the lab write-up on page 171 of the Surviving a Science Fair Project section and go shopping.

3. Assemble the materials and perform the lab at least once. Gather as much data as you can.

4. Go to page 148 and read the material. Then start on Step 1 of Preparing Your Science Fair Project. With any luck you can dodge an academic disaster.

___ **B. I am worm bait.** My science fair project is due tomorrow and there is not anything moldy in the fridge. I need a big Band-Aid, in a hurry.

Directions: Same as Option A. You can decide if and when you want to clue your folks in on your current dilemma.

___ **C. I am the parent of a student who informed me that he/she has been assigned a science fair project due in six to eight weeks.** My son/daughter has expressed an interest in science books with humorous illustrations that attempt to explain chemistry and associated ideas.

Who Are You ? And ...

Directions: Well, you came to the right place. Give your kid these directions and stand back.

1. The first step is to read through the Table of Contents and see if anything grabs your interest. Read through several experiments, see if the science teacher has any of the more difficult-to-acquire-materials, like diffraction gratings, polarizing filters, and some of the chemicals, and ask if they can be borrowed. Play with the experiments and see which one really tickles your fancy.

2. After you have found and conducted an experiment that you like, take a peek at the Science Fair Ideas and see if you would like to investigate one of those or create an idea of your own. The guidelines for those are listed in the Science Fair section. You have plenty of time so you can fiddle and fool with the original experiment and its derivations several times. Work until you have an original question you want to answer and then start the process. You are well on your way to an excellent grade.

___D. I am a responsible student and have been assigned a science fair project due in six to eight weeks. I am interested in chemistry, and despite demonstrating maturity and wisdom well beyond the scope of my peers, I too still have a sense of humor. Enlighten and entertain me.

Directions: Cool. Being teachers, we have heard reports of this kind of thing happening but usually in an obscure and hard-to-locate town several states removed. Nonetheless, congratulations.

Same as Option C. You have plenty of time and should be able to score very well. We'll keep our eyes peeled when the Nobel Prizes are announced in a couple of decades.

How to Use This Book

___**E. I am a parent who home schools my child/children.** We are always on the lookout for quality curriculum materials that are not only educationally sound but also kid- and teacher-friendly. I am not particularly strong in science, but I realize it is a very important topic. How is this book going to help me out?

Directions: In a lot of ways we created this book specifically for home schoolers.

1. We have taken the National Content Standards, the guidelines that are used by all public and private schools nationwide to establish their curriculum base, and listed them in the Table of Contents. You now know where you stand with respect to the national standards.

2. We then break these standards down and list the major ideas that you should want your kid to know. We call these the Big Ideas. Some people call them objectives, others call them curriculum standards, educational benchmarks, or assessment norms. Same apple, different name. The bottom line is that when your children are done studying this unit on chemistry, you want them not only to understand and explain each of the 8 Big Ideas listed in this book, but also, to be able to defend and argue their position based on experiential evidence.

3. Building on the Big Ideas, we have collected and rewritten 50 hands-on science labs. Each one has been specifically selected so that it supports the Big Idea that it is correlated to. This is critical. As the kids do the science experiment, they see, smell, touch, and hear the experiment. They will store that information in several places in their brains. When it comes time to comprehend the Big Idea, the concrete hands-on experiences provide the foundation for building the Idea, which is quite often abstract. Kids who merely read about density gradients, physical vs. chemical changes, and bipolar molecules, or who see pictures of emulsions, suspensions, and colloids but have never squeezed them between their fingers, are trying to build abstract ideas on abstract ideas and quite often miss the mark.

Who Are You ? And ...

For example: I can show you a recipe in a book for chocolate chip cookies and ask you to reiterate it. Or I can turn you loose in a kitchen, have you mix the ingredients, grease the pan, plop the dough on the cookie sheet, slide everything into the oven, and wait impatiently until they pop out eight minutes later. Chances are that the description given by the person who actually made the cookies is going to be much clearer because it is based on true understanding of the process, because it is based on experience.

4. Once students have completed the experiment, there are a number of extension ideas under the Science Fair Extensions that allow them to spend as much or as little time on the ideas as they deem necessary.

5. A word about humor. Science is not usually known for being funny even though Bill Nye, The Science Guy, Beaker from Sesame Street, and Beakman's World do their best to mingle the two. That's all fine and dandy, but we want you to know that we incorporate humor because it is scientifically (and educationally) sound to do so. Plus it's really at the root of our personalities. Here's what we know:

When we laugh ...

a. Our pupils dilate, increasing the amount of light entering the eye.

b. Our heart rate increases, which pumps more blood to the brain.

c. Oxygen-rich blood to the brain means the brain is able to collect, process, and store more information. Big I.E.: increased comprehension.

d. Laughter relaxes muscles, which can be involuntarily tense if a student is uncomfortable or fearful of an academic topic.

e. Laughter stimulates the immune system, which will ultimately translate into overall health and fewer kids who say they are sick of science.

f. Socially, it provides an acceptable pause in the academic routine, which then gives students time to regroup and prepare to address some of the more difficult ideas with a renewed spirit. They can study longer and focus on ideas more efficiently.

g. Laughter releases chemicals in the brain that are associated with pleasure and joy.

6. If you follow the book in the order it is written, you will be able to build ideas and concepts in a logical and sequential pattern. But that is by no means necessary. For a complete set of guidelines on our ideas on how to teach home-schooled kids science, check out our book, Why's the Cat on Fire? How to Excel at Teaching Science to Your Home-Schooled Kids.

How to Use This Book

___ **F.** **I am a public/private school teacher,** and this looks like an interesting book to add ideas to my classroom lesson plans.

Directions: It is, and please feel free to do so. However, while this is a great classroom resource for kids, may we also recommend several other titles: What's It Matter? *(Basic Intro to Chemistry),* The Labware Jungle *(Learning to ID & Use Labware),* Snot In a Box, *(Polymers & Colloids),* A pH Primer *(Acids, Bases, & pH),* and Soup, Goop and Other Poop *(Mixtures, Emulsions, & Solutions),* and That's the Point *(Solids, Liquids, & Gas).*

These books have teacher-preparation pages, student-response sheets or lab pages, lesson plans, bulletin board ideas, discovery center ideas, vocabulary sheets, unit pretests, unit exams, lab practical exams, and student grading sheets — basically everything you need if you are a science nincompoop, and a couple of cool ideas if you are a seasoned veteran with an established curriculum. All of the ideas that are covered in this one book are covered much more thoroughly in the others. They were specifically written for teachers.

___ **G.** **My son/daughter/grandson/niece/father-in-law is interested in science, and this looks like fun.**

Directions: Congratulations on your selection. Add a gift certificate to the local science supply store and a package of hot chocolate mix and you have the perfect rainy Saturday afternoon gig.

___ **H.** **My cooking class is concerned about the decomposition of fatty acids in a high pH environment, in particular, with respect to the role of bonding sites relative to temperature sensitivity. Can you help?**

Directions: Nope. Try the Sous Chef down the street.

Lab Safety

Contained herein are 50 science activities to help you better understand the nature and characteristics of chemicals as we currently understand these things. However, since you are on your own in this journey, we thought it prudent to share some basic wisdom and experience in the safety department.

Read the Instructions

An interesting concept, especially if you are a teenager. Take a minute before you jump in and get going to read all of the instructions as well as warnings. If you do not understand something, stop and ask an adult for help.

Clean Up All Messes

Keep your lab area clean. It will make it easier to put everything away at the end and may also prevent contamination and the subsequent germination of a species of mutant tomato bug larva. You will also find that chemicals perform with more predictability if they are not poisoned with foreign molecules.

Organize

Translation: Put it back where you get it. If you need any more clarification, there is an opening at the landfill for you.

HELLO.

GOODBYE.

Dispose of Poisons Properly

This will not be much of a problem with the labs that are suggested in this book. However, if you happen to wander over into one of the many disciplines that incorporates the use of more advanced chemicals, then we would suggest that you use great caution with the materials and definitely dispose of any and all poisons properly.

Practice Good Fire Safety

If there is a fire in the room, notify an adult immediately. If an adult is not in the room and the fire is manageable, smother the outbreak with a fire blanket or use a fire extinguisher. When the fire is contained, immediately send someone to find an adult. If, for any reason, you happen to catch on fire, **REMEMBER: Stop, Drop, and Roll.** Never run; it adds oxygen to the fire, making it burn faster, and it also scares the bat guano out of the neighbors when they see the neighbor kids running down the block doing an imitation of a campfire marshmallow without the stick.

Protect Your Skin

It is a good idea to always wear protective gloves whenever you are working with chemicals. Again, this particular book does not suggest or incorporate hazardous chemicals in its lab activities. We are primarily using only safe, manageable kinds of chemicals for these labs. If you do happen to spill a chemical on your skin, notify an adult immediately and then flush the area with water for 15 minutes. It's unlikely, but if irritation develops, have your parent or another responsible adult look at it. If it appears to be of concern, contact a physician. Take any information that you have about the chemical with you.

Lab Safety

Save Your Nose Hairs

Sounds like a cause celebre L.A. style, but it is really good advice. To smell a chemical to identify it, hold the open container six to ten inches down and away from your nose. Make a clockwise circular motion with your hand over the opening of the container, "wafting" some of the fumes toward your nose. This will allow you to safely smell some of the fumes without exposing yourself to a large dose of anything noxious. This technique may help prevent a nosebleed or your lungs from accidentally getting burned.

Wear Goggles If Appropriate

If the lab asks you to heat or mix chemicals, be sure to wear protective eyewear. Also have an eyewash station or running water available. You never know when something is going to splatter, splash, or react unexpectedly. It is better to look like a nerd and be prepared than schedule a trip down to pick out a Seeing Eye dog. If you do happen to accidentally get chemicals in your eye, flush the area for 15 minutes. If any irritation or pain develops, immediately go see a doctor.

Lose the Comedy Routine

You should have plenty of time scheduled during your day to mess around, but science lab is not one of them. Horseplay breaks glassware, spills chemicals, and creates unnecessary messes— things that parents do not appreciate. Trust us on this one.

No Eating

Do not eat while performing a lab. Putting your food in the lab area contaminates your food and the experiment. This makes for bad science and worse indigestion. Avoid poisoning yourself and goobering up your labware by observing this rule.

Happy and safe experimenting!

Recommended Materials Suppliers

For every lesson in this book, we offer a list of materials. Many of these are very easy to acquire, and if you do not have them in your home already, you will be able to find them at the local grocery or hardware store. For more difficult items, we have selected, for your convenience, a small but respectable list of suppliers who will meet your needs in a timely and economical manner. Call for a catalog or quote on the item that you are looking for, and they will be happy to give you a hand.

Loose in the Lab
9462 South 560 West
Sandy, UT 84070
Phone 1-888-403-1189
Fax 1-801-568-9586
www.looseinthelab.com

Delta Education
80 NW Blvd.
Nashua, NH 03063
Phone 1-800-442-5444
Fax 1-800-282-9560
www.delta-education.com

Nasco
901 Jonesville Ave.
Fort Atkinson, WI 53538
Phone 1-414-563-2446
Fax 1-920-563-8296
www.nascofa.com

Ward's Scientific
5100 W Henrietta Rd.
Rochester, NY 14692
Phone 1-800-387-7822
Fax 1-716-334-6174
www.wardsci.com

Educational Innovations
151 River Rd.
Cos Cob, CT 06807
Phone 1-888-912-7474
Fax 1-203-629-2739
www.teachersource.com

Frey Scientific
100 Paragon Pkwy.
Mansfield, OH 44903
Phone 1-800-225-FREY
Fax 1-419-589-1546
www.freyscientific.com

Fisher Scientific
485 S. Frontage Rd.
Burr Ridge, IL 60521
Phone 1-800-955-1177
Fax 1-800-955-0740
www.fisheredu.com

Flinn Scientific
PO Box 219
Batavia, IL 60510
Phone 1-800-452-1261
Fax 1-630-879-6962
www.flinnsci.com

The Ideas,
Lab Activities,
& Science Fair
Extensions

Big Idea 1

Each kind of matter has a unique set of properties that allows the chemist to identify that matter. These properties include solubility, density, magnetism, flame test color, and melting point, which are all independent of the size of the sample.

Purple Streamers

The Experiment

The first characteristic that we are going to take a look at is solubility of certain chemicals and compounds in water.

If chemicals are soluble, they will begin to break apart, dissolve, and appear smaller in size. Curiously enough, some chemicals will leave a trail in the water as they dissolve. We are going to introduce you to one of those chemicals.

We would also like to take this opportunity to debunk the boyhood myth that young men between the ages of 4 and 10 will actually melt when they come in contact with water. The same is true of little old ladies with foul dispositions dressed as witches in classic movies.

Materials

1	Toobe
	or
1	Large drinking glass
1	Paper clip
1	Plastic pen cap
1	Vial of potassium permanganate
1	Pair of tweezers
1	Pair of gloves (recommended)
	Water

Procedure

1. Fill the Toobe with warm water. Drop the paper clip into the water and observe what, if anything, happens to the size of the clip. Record your observations in the data table below.

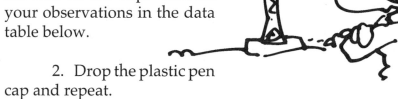

2. Drop the plastic pen cap and repeat.

3. Finally, use the pair of tweezers to pick up a large crystal of potassium permanganate and drop it into the water. Observe what happens to the chemical as it comes in contact with the water and falls to the bottom of the Toobe. Record your observations.

Data & Observations

Object	Material	Dissolved? Y/N
Paper clip	Iron	
Pen cap	Plastic	
Crystal	Potassium Permanganate	

How Come, Huh?

The crystal is made of billions of potassium permanganate atoms stacked together in a uniform pattern. The bonds holding these atoms together are not strong enough to withstand the bouncing and banging of the water molecules as the crystal enters the water. Therefore, they get knocked apart. When they get separated from the surface of the crystal, they are free to hang around in the water and make new friends.

Double Occupancy

The Experiment

Matter takes up space, and no two pieces of matter can occupy the same space. Or can they?

Well, no. Technically this is not possible, but you can create the illusion by using two liquids that are miscible. By miscible we mean that the total volume of the two is less than the sum of the two separate liquids. Zen chemistry? No, but slightly confusing, maybe. Try this.

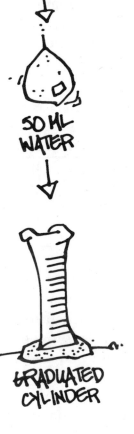

Materials

1   Gallon jar
10 Tennis balls or racquet balls
100 Marbles
1   Wax cup
1   100 mL graduated cylinder
     50 mL isopropyl alcohol
     50 mL water

Procedure

1. Measure 50 mL of water into a graduated cylinder and then pour it into a wax cup.

2. Measure 50 mL of isopropyl alcohol and add it to the graduated cylinder. Now add the 50 mL of water from the wax cup. Read the total volume of liquid in the graduated cylinder.

3. Add the tennis balls (representing the alcohol molecules) to the gallon jar. Once they are in the jar, add the marbles (representing the water molecules) one at a time and observe how they move when they are "poured" into the container.

How Come, Huh?

Isopropyl alcohol and water are miscible. What this means is that when you add 50 mL of alcohol to 50 mL of water, instead of getting 100 mL of combined liquid, you get a volume that is slightly less.

Logic tells you that this is impossible. No two chunks, blobs, or molecules of matter can take up the same space. To find out why, we have to turn to our tennis ball/marble model.

Alcohol molecules (tennis balls) are huge; water molecules (marbles) are much smaller. When you added the alcohol to the graduated cylinder, there were lots of small spaces left between these huge molecules— spaces just big enough for a water molecule (marble) to wiggle into and take up residence in. Because the water molecules are filling in the spaces left by the large molecules, the total volume appears to be less than what it should be, but it isn't.

Frosty Coffee

The Experiment
You are going to use the process of sublimation to create crystals that can be seen with the naked eye. Sublimation is a term chemists use when chemicals and compounds change directly from solids to gases, or vice-versa, without bothering to pass through a liquid state. In this experiment, caffeine sublimates at about 178°C. The caffeine, once in a gas state, condenses and forms pure, small, white, needle-like crystals of caffeine.

Materials
1   16 mm x 150 mm test tube
1   20 mm x 150 mm test tube
1   Votive candle
1   Book of matches
1   Hand lens
1   Wood splint
    Approx. 0.25g caffeine powder

Procedure
1.   Grab the caffeine, measure out a quarter of a gram, and dump it into the bottom of the larger of the two test tubes.

2.   Slide the smaller test tube into the larger one so that the bottom of the small test tube is about 1 inch from the caffeine in the bottom of the large test tube. Use the illustration at the right as a guide.

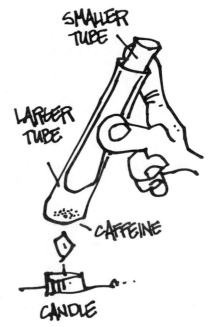

3.   With adult supervision, light the candle. Hold the two test tubes just above the top of the flame. You will notice that some of the caffeine immediately starts to melt, vaporize, and then recrystallize on the smaller test tube inside the larger one. As you continue to heat the two tubes, the remainder of the caffeine will sublimate into a gas and will deposit itself onto the surface of the smaller tube.

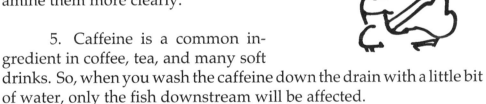

4.   After three or four minutes, carefully remove the small test tube and look at the newly formed caffeine crystals on the bottom of it. This is where the hand lens comes in handy. Take the wood splint and pull out some of the long needles from inside the test tube. These are very fine crystals. The hand lens allows you to examine them more clearly.

5.   Caffeine is a common ingredient in coffee, tea, and many soft drinks. So, when you wash the caffeine down the drain with a little bit of water, only the fish downstream will be affected.

How Come, Huh?

When the caffeine molecules get enough energy to turn to a vapor, they rise into the air above the liquid and cool very quickly— so quickly, in fact, that they do not have time to turn to a liquid again before becoming a solid. They lose the heat energy and immediately find their buddies that are forming crystals on the test tube. They join them.

Mini Lava Lamp

The Experiment

This lab introduces several concepts: solubility, density, and states of matter—all of which tie into our Big Idea of learning to identify the specific characteristics of individual elements.

Materials

1   Preform tube w/ cap
1   Bottle of cooking oil
1   Package of Tubtints
    Water

Procedure

1. Fill the preform tube four-fifths full with cooking oil.

2. Slowly add water to the side of the pre-form tube until the level of the liquid comes right to the top. Observe the water as it sinks to the bottom of the tube. Continue to observe the water blobs as they combine and unite at the bottom of the tube.

3. When you have one big blob of water at the bottom of the tube, open the Tubtints and select a tablet. Drop the tablet into the tube and watch it as it falls through the oil and hits the pocket of water at the bottom of the tube.

4. The minute the Tubtint hits the water, it should start to fizz and bubble. Observe what happens to the water as the Tubtint dissolves.

5. Observe the tube until all of the fizzing stops. Let the bubbles of colored water collect on the bottom of the tube. When they recombine to make a large bubble, screw the cap back on the tube.

6. Gently tip the tube back and forth and observe the movement of the water and the oil.

How Come, Huh?

There are several things going on here. We will tackle each of them separately.

A. The water sinks to the bottom of the tube because it is denser than the oil. Another way of putting this is that water molecules are packed tighter than oil molecules, something we explored in the Double Occupancy lab. The water falls to the bottom of the tube and displaces, or pushes up on, the oil.

B. The Tubtints are made of a water-soluble chemical. When they come in contact with the oil, they do not react with it; they simply fall through it until they hit the water. When they hit the water, they react by dissolving, which releases a dye into the water and emits bubbles of gas.

C. The bubbles of gas cling to the bubbles of water. This is like putting a little tiny life jacket on each blob of water. The water becomes more buoyant and rises toward the top of the tube. When the water blob hits the surface of the oil, the gas bubbles are released from the water blob and go into the atmosphere. When this happens, the water bubbles all of a sudden become denser again and sink back down to the bottom of the tube.

Mini Lava Lamp

D. When the Tubtint has completely reacted with the water, the tube can be tipped back and forth. The water, which is denser than the oil, always responds to the pull of gravity and displaces the oil so that it can move. The thick nature of the liquids, relative to the air, makes it appear as if the water is forming a wave that is rolling back and forth inside the tube.

E. Finally, the reason that the Tubtint only dyed the water a color and not the oil as well is that it is a water-soluble compound—meaning that it will break apart and dissolve in the presence of water but not oil.

Demagnetizing Iron

The Experiment

A few elements respond to magnetic fields. This is a defining characteristic. In this lab, you are going to show that sometimes the defining characteristic of an element or compound is lost when a new compound is formed.

Materials

1	16 mm x 150 mm test tube
1	Votive candle
1	Book of matches
1	Hammer
1	Napkin
1	Pair of goggles
1	Bottle of iron filings
1	Bottle of sulfur powder
1	Ceramic magnet
1	Wood splint
2	Baggies
	Adult Supervision

Procedure

1. Goggles on. Pour a small sample of iron filings out onto a baggie that has been placed on the tabletop. Place the ceramic magnet in the second baggie and bring it close to the pile of iron filings. Observe what happens to the filings.

2. Repeat this procedure with a small pile of sulfur and the magnet. You should notice that the iron filings are attracted to the magnet and the sulfur is not. Record this observation in the data table on page 33.

Demagnetizing Iron

3. Fold the baggie and pour the iron and sulfur that you tested into the test tube.

4. Place your thumb over the end of the tube and shake the two elements together until you have a mixture of iron and sulfur. Pour the mixture back out onto the baggie and test the mixture to see if it is attracted to the magnet. Record your observation in the data table on the next page.

5. Pour the mixture back in the test tube and light the candle. Did we mention goggles? Time to put them back on, even if they have fogged up.

6. Heat the iron and sulfur mixture in the flame of the candle. Rotate the bottom of the tube in the flame and watch to see that the sulfur starts to melt. Continue to heat the two elements for 3 minutes after you first notice signs of the sulfur melting. By doing so, you'll produce iron sulfide.

7. Be especially careful here. Wrap the test tube in a napkin and gently hit it with the hammer, breaking the glass. Carefully remove the glass and test the new compound, iron sulfide, with the magnet wrapped in the baggie. Record your new observation in the data table on the next page.

Data & Observations

Item Tested	Type	Magnetic? Y/N
Iron Filings	Element	
Sulfur Powder	Element	
Iron/Sulfur	Mixture	
Iron Sulfide	Compound	

How Come, Huh?

We have four separate tests, so we will explain them one at a time, starting with the iron filings:

A. Iron filings are naturally magnetic, so when the magnet was brought near the element, it was attracted to the magnet.

B. Sulfur is not magnetic and, as a consequence, it did not respond to the magnet.

C. When the sulfur and iron were tumbled around in the tube, you made a mixture. A mixture is a collection of two or more things, side by side but not connected in any way to one another. As the magnet was brought near the mixture, the iron was attracted to it; the sulfur, which was not attracted to the magnet, was left behind.

D. By heating the iron and sulfur together, you provided enough energy for the two to combine and form a new compound, iron sulfide. A compound is created when two or more elements are hooked together, forming a new compound that has its own new and unique set of characteristics. The iron lost its magnetism when it combined with the sulfur.

Metal Flame Test

The Experiment

This activity will allow you to see the "fingerprints" of a variety of chemicals. The light we see from one chemical when it is introduced into a flame may be different from the light emitted by another chemical. By using diffraction grating glasses, you will learn about identifying different chemical light sources by their "fingerprints."

Spectroscopes have a special diffraction grating film that acts like a prism and separates light into its colors. Different elements combine to make different light emissions. These different combinations of elements make color patterns, called spectra, that are unique to the different chemicals. By using diffraction grating glasses, you can identify mystery substances and investigate unknown compounds.

Materials

1   Pair of diffraction grating glasses
1   Propane torch
1   Nichrome wire
1   Bottle of 10% hydrochloric acid
1   Bottle of barium chloride
1   Bottle of potassium chloride
1   Bottle of strontium chloride
Adult Supervision

Procedure

1. Place the propane torch in a open area. Use all fire safety procedures.

2. Dip the nichrome wire into the acid and then introduce it into the flame. You'll notice that the acid cleans the gunk off the wire. You should also notice that the nichrome wire does not change the appearance of the propane flame. This is important.

3. Put on your diffraction grating glasses. Dip the end of a newly cleaned nichrome wire into the barium chloride. Hold the salts (the crystals you just picked up) in the flame and observe the color that is produced. Repeat the experiment with your diffraction grating glasses off. Record your observations in the data table below.

4. Repeat this procedure for the other two chemicals. Record your observations.

Data & Observations

Chemical Tested	Flame Test Colors	
	Naked Eye	Diffraction Grating
Barium Chloride		
Potassium Chloride		
Strontium Chloride		

Metal Flame Test

How Come, Huh?

When an element or compound is placed in a flame, it produces light. Each element and compound produces a light that is different when viewed through a spectroscope. Spectroscopes and diffraction grating glasses take the light and split it into the different colors of the rainbow, displaying them as bands of red, orange, yellow, and the like. This combination of color bands produces a unique color "fingerprint" that only one specific compound produces. The cool thing about this is that this technique can be used to identify mystery substances and unknown compounds.

Astronomers use the light received through spectroscopes to learn about objects in space. This light carries information about a star's temperature, composition, magnetic fields, and motion. This information is decoded by splitting the light into a spectrum using a spectroscope. The bright line spectrum that results is often called an emission spectrum or a characteristic spectrum. Every atom has an individual and characteristic spectrum, much like every person has a fingerprint that is like no other and can be used for identification.

Big Idea 2

Matter can exist in three different states: solid, liquid, or gas. Matter changes state when the temperature goes up or down. If matter changes state directly from solid to gas or from gas to solid, it is said to be undergoing the process of sublimation. Carbon dioxide is an excellent example of a compound that sublimates at room temperature.

Dry Ice Primer

What is Dry Ice?

Dry ice is carbon dioxide gas that is solidified by using a combination of low temperature and pressure to compress it into a solid. It looks like ice but "smokes" immediately when it is exposed to air. This smoke is water vapor that is being condensed when it comes in contact with the very cold carbon dioxide gas. The smoke is harmless and generally disappears as soon as it warms to room temperature.

Where Do I get Dry Ice?

The first place to check is the local grocery store. If that does not work out, try the local veterinary clinic, ice cream parlor, or meat packing plant. Still no dry ice? Check with hospitals, emergency clinics, and if all else fails, look under **Dry Ice** in the Yellow Pages of your phone directory.

Dry ice sells for around 60 to 80 cents a pound, and you do not need a permit, valid driver's license, or mandate from a Federal authority to buy or transport the stuff.

How Do I Handle Dry Ice?

Very carefully. It is extremely cold—112° below zero, to be exact. Even brief contact with skin can cause the cells to freeze solid and die. The best way to handle the stuff is to wear a pair of cotton gloves and get the dry ice wrapped in paper as quickly as possible.

How Do I Transport Dry Ice?

If you are going a short distance, toss it in paper, wrap it as tightly as you can, and then place it in a cooler that has a drain spout in the bottom. Keep the spout open.

The one big mistake that you can make is to place the dry ice in a thermos or other closed container (cooler with a closed drain spout) and then seal it shut. The dry ice starts to sublimate rapidly at room temperature and the container will increase in gas pressure. You must allow for the gas to be released. This is extremely important for your safety.

How Do I Store Dry Ice?

If you need to keep dry ice for a period of time, wrap it in paper and then place it in a cooler that has a drain spout in the bottom. Keep the spout open. If you can place the dry ice in your freezer at home, that also helps. As a general rule, 10 pounds keeps for about 1 day.

How Do I Prepare Dry Ice?

When you are ready to perform the lab activities, take a hammer and gently whap the dry ice while it is still wrapped in the paper. After several good smacks, unwrap the paper, put your gloves on, and distribute the pieces.

How Do I Dispose of Dry Ice?

You can just let it sublimate until it is all gone during your lab. If you overestimated your needs, you can get rid of it in a number of ways, including:

A. Toss it in a sink and let it dissipate.

B. Get a large bowl, fill it with hot water, and make a "Witches Brew" that bubbles and boils.

C. Our favorite use of extra dry ice is to head for the bathroom and toss it in the commode. Nothing like a smoking, boiling toilet to make you wonder what the person just ahead of you ate for lunch.

D. NEVER, EVER SUCK ON DRY ICE LIKE A REGULAR PIECE OF ICE.

Fog City

The Experiment

This is one of my favorite experiments, simply because it really looks like you are doing science. You have a tube, it is full of liquid that is bubbling, fog is boiling over the edge, and you can just bet that Dr. Frankenstein is going to walk around the corner any second.

Materials

1   Toobe
    or
1   Drinking glass, large
1   Bottle of liquid detergent
1   Chunk of dry ice
    Water
    Adult Supervision

Procedure

1. Fill the Toobe three-fourths full of water. Warm water accelerates the reaction and produces more fog faster than cool water does.

2. Drop a couple of chunks of dry ice into the Toobe and enjoy the show.

How Come, Huh?

The dry ice immediately sublimates in the bottom of the Toobe, changing from a solid to a gas. This gas is much less dense than the water, so it rises quickly to the top of the container. When the cold gas comes in contact with the warm air, it causes the moisture in the air to condense. This is the fog you see. The condensed air is mixed with the carbon dioxide. It is heavier than the surrounding air and falls to the ground. As the condensed air warms up, it evaporates quickly.

Dry Ice Cannon

The Experiment

This is a great way to have more fun with one of our favorite compounds. A small piece of dry ice is placed in a test tube and stoppered. The dry ice immediately starts to sublimate, producing a loud "pop" and flying stoppers.

Materials

1   20 mm x 150 mm test tube
1   Stopper, solid rubber, #1
1   Chunk of dry ice
1   Pair of goggles
    Adult Supervision

Procedure

1. Goggles on. Place several small pieces of dry ice in the bottom of the test tube.

2. Insert the stopper firmly into the mouth of the test tube and wait 15 to 30 seconds. Don't look directly at the stopper or point it at anyone in the room.

How Come, Huh?

When the stopper is inserted into the mouth of the tube, you create a closed system. As the dry ice sublimates, the gas pressure inside the tube gets higher and higher until something has to give. That something is the stopper. The pressure shoves the stopper out of the tube rapidly, the gas expands causing a soundwave or "pop," and the pressure goes back to normal.

Squealing George

The Experiment

This lab also doubles as an opportunity to study sound and, if you want to have a little fun, you can tell your friends that George Washington got so cold crossing the Delaware that, to this very day, you can hear his teeth chatter.

Materials

1   Flat piece of dry ice
1   Quarter, U.S.
1   Pair of cotton gloves
1   Coffee mug
    Very hot water

Procedure

1. Put the gloves on. Find a piece of dry ice that has at least one flat edge. Place the dry ice in the palm of your hand.

2. Remove the glove that is not holding the dry ice and pick up the quarter. Take note of the temperature of the coin. Put your glove back on.

3. Place the quarter, face down, on the dry ice. Then press. You should hear a loud squealing sound for 5 to 10 seconds.

4. Once the squealing has ended, remove the quarter from the dry ice and remove the cotton glove from the hand that is not holding the dry ice. Touch the quarter and compare the current temperature with the starting temperature.

5. Drop the quarter into a cup of very hot water and let it heat up for about 30 seconds. Remove the quarter and place it on the dry ice. Compare the loudness of the sound that you hear as well as the length of time that the quarter squeals.

How Come, Huh?

The piece of dry ice is constantly producing gas at room temperature. When you placed the quarter on the dry ice, you trapped the escaping gas under the surface of the quarter. The gas did not like this, so it pushed up on the quarter to get out. As soon as it escaped, the quarter dropped back down and trapped more gas. In real time, this produced a very rapidly vibrating quarter that created the squeal you heard.

The quarter was also losing heat to the dry ice and becoming very cool. Metal is an excellent conductor of heat and, when the temperature of the metal approached the temperature of the dry ice, the carbon dioxide thought it was insulated by a layer of cold metal, so it stopped producing gas. No gas, no squealing.

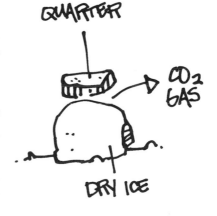

Finally, the reason we had you heat the quarter was to see that the hotter the quarter is, the faster the reaction and the louder the squeal will be. Temperature affects chemical reactions this way.

The Invisible Fire Extinguisher

The Experiment

Carbon dioxide is not flammable. In fact, it is used in fire extinguishers because it is actually very effective at putting fires out. This lab will allow you to demonstrate this characteristic of carbon dioxide, as well as its density, relative to air.

Materials

1   Chunk of dry ice
2   Large drinking glasses
1   Votive candle
1   Book of matches
    Adult Supervision

Procedure

1. Place one of the empty drinking glasses in front of you. With the assistance of an adult, light a match and slowly lower it into the cup as far as you can. Watch to see if the match is extinguished at any point in time as you lower it into the cup.

2. Plop a chunk of dry ice into the same cup and let it sit there for 30 seconds. Carefully light a second match and slowly lower it into the cup. Compare the results this time with the first time you lowered the match.

3. Light the candle. Gently pour some of the carbon dioxide gas out of the cup and over the flame. Use the illustration above as a guide to help you. Imagine that the cup is full of water. The gas behaves in the same fashion as water does. It extinguishes the flame.

4. Relight the candle. Pour carbon dioxide from the first cup that has the dry ice in it into the second, empty cup. Now take the "empty" cup and gently pour the carbon dioxide over the candle. Observe what happens to the flame.

How Come, Huh?

Carbon dioxide is heavier than air. When the gas sublimates, it collects inside the cup. As you lowered the match into the gas, the flame was extinguished at the level of the carbon dioxide.

You were able to pour the carbon dioxide from cup to cup because it is heavier than air. When the gas is poured from the cup onto the candle flame, it pushes the air out of the way, and the flame goes out.

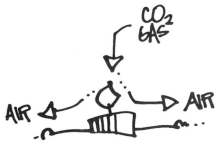

The Bubble Machine

The Experiment

The entertainment never stops. You are going to take some easy-to-acquire household materials and make a bubble machine that produces large, smoky, carbon-dioxide-filled bubbles.

Materials

1   Half-gallon, plastic jar w/lid
1   Marking pen, fine
1   #2, 1-hole stopper, rubber
1   Router *or*
1   X-Acto knife
1   18 inch length of copper tubing
1   Square of fabric, 2 inches x 6 inches
1   Rubber band
1   Bottle of bubble solution
1   Chunk of dry ice
     Water

Procedure

1.   Place the stopper, narrow end down, in the center of the lid of the plastic jar. Using the marking pen, trace around the base of the stopper. Use the illustration at the right as a guide.

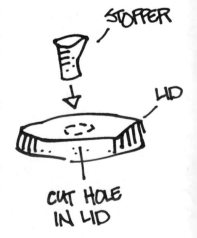

2.   Carefully remove the center of the lid, using the router or X-Acto knife.

3.   Unroll about 10 inches of the copper tubing. Dip the end in bubble solution and insert 1 inch into the stopper.

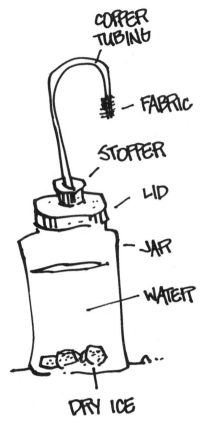

COPPER TUBING

FABRIC

STOPPER

LID

JAR

WATER

DRY ICE

4. Finish unrolling the copper tubing and form a large "U" at the end of it, as in the illustration at the left. Insert the stopper into the lid.

5. Wrap the other end of the copper tubing with fabric, and hold it in place with a rubber band. Do not cover the opening of the tube; just wrap around it.

6. Fill the jar three-fourths full with warm water. Drop in four pieces of dry ice. Quickly screw the lid onto the jar and make sure the stopper sits firmly in the hole.

7. Dip the fabric end of the wire into the soap bubble solution and observe what happens when the carbon dioxide is pushed up through the tube and fills the soap solution drip.

8. Get your hands wet and attempt to catch the soap bubbles that form and drop from the tubing. If they break, open your fingers slightly and let the smoke drip through them.

The Bubble Machine

9. Keep the bubbles flowing by dipping the fabric into the soap solution and adding more dry ice to the jar.

How Come, Huh?

The dry ice immediately started to sublimate and change from a solid to a gas. This filled the top portion of the plastic jar with carbon dioxide. As more and more carbon dioxide enters the top half of the jar, the higher the pressure gets. Eventually the gas is going to get shoved up and around the tube.

The soap solution is a heavy, thick liquid that drips down the fabric as gravity tugs on it. When it gets to the bottom of the fabric, it naturally fills the hole in the end of the copper tubing. As the gas is pushed through the hole in the tubing by the pressure inside the plastic jar, it fills and stretches the soap drip into a bubble.

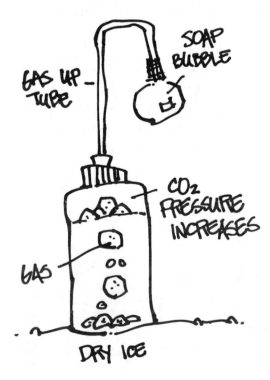

GAS UP TUBE

SOAP BUBBLE

CO₂ PRESSURE INCREASES

GAS

DRY ICE

The bubble continues to fill with carbon dioxide and eventually gets too heavy to be supported by the molecules connecting it to the copper tubing. At this point, it falls to the ground.

If you are lucky enough to catch the bubble whole, you can play with it for a while. However, the soap solution will continue to flow and will weaken the bubble until it bursts. The carbon dioxide and water vapor solution drizzles through your fingers because it is heavier than air.

Big Idea 3

EXOTHERMIC.
DEFINITELY,
EXOTHERMIC.

Some chemicals release heat when they react with other compounds. These reactions are called exothermic reactions. Other chemicals absorb heat when they react with certain chemicals. These reactions are called endothermic reactions.

plock Handwarmer

The Experiment

Two chemicals will be mixed in a sealed container. When the gas pressure increases to the point where the container fails, we will have a small and very polite explosion of gas.

Materials

1   Measuring cup
1   1 oz. bottle of sodium bicarbonate (baking soda powder)
1   1 oz. bottle of calcium chloride
1   Resealable baggie
    Water

Procedure

1.   Add a half-cup of warm water to the baggie. If you don't have a measuring cup, fill the bag until there is about an inch of water in it. **(Be sure to use warm water. Using cold water will change the experiment significantly.)**

2.   Remove the cap from the calcium chloride bottle and add about one-third of the bottle to the water. Zip the baggie closed and roll the calcium chloride pellets between your fingertips. As the chemical starts to dissolve, you should notice a significant increase in temperature, particularly as you rub the pellets.

3.   Open the baggie, add one-third of the bottle of sodium bicarbonate powder, and *quickly* zip the baggie closed again. Observe what happens when the chemicals come in contact and react with each other.

CALCIUM
CHLORIDE

WATER

BAGGIE

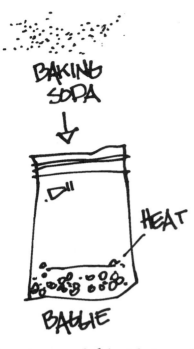

BAKING SODA

HEAT

BAGGIE

4. As the reaction proceeds, hold the baggie up to your ear and listen. The bag will swell with gas until it "pops" along the zipper. You can either close it up and let it collect more gas or …

5. Pour the ingredients down the drain with lots of running water.

How Come, Huh?

When calcium chloride is mixed with water, it splits apart, forming calcium ions and chloride ions. When this happens, the energy that was holding those atoms together is released as heat. That is why the bag started to feel warm as the reaction proceeded.

Once the chemicals have split apart, each chemical is free to react with other chemicals, like the sodium bicarbonate powder. The chloride reacts with the sodium in the sodium bicarbonate to form table salt and carbon dioxide, which is a gas. A gas takes up more space than a liquid, and this extra gas causes the bag to swell.

As the amount of gas inside the bag increases, the pressure also increases. All of this gas pressure puts considerable strain on the plastic lock that is holding everything inside the bag. When the pressure gets to be too much, the lock gives, and the gas rushes out, rapidly producing a "boom."

Surprise Fire

The Experiment

This lab is in a virtual dead heat with the Cornstarch Explosion as my all-time favorite. The only thing really separating the two is that the Cornstarch Explosion was the very first experiment that I did for my students when I started teaching. For that reason, it will always be a favorite.

This lab is an excellent demonstration of volcanos, if such a Science Fair project strikes your fancy. It is also a good way to show change of state. Finally, it is one of the best experiments in the book for stinking up your house. So, go outside.

Materials

1   Bottle of glycerine
1   Bottle of potassium permanganate
2   Pairs of goggles
1   Tart pan
1   Napkin
    Water
    Adult Supervision

GLYCERINE

POTASSIUM PERMANGANATE

TART PAN

Procedure

1. Place a wet paper towel under an inverted tart pan in a **well ventilated** area. Make a small volcano in the center of the tart pan using potassium permanganate. The volcano should be no more than two inches in diameter.

2. Make a hole in the center of the volcano with your thumb and carefully fill the hole with glycerine until it starts to flow down the side of the volcano. Wait 15 to 30 seconds and the show will begin.

3. There will be a poof of smoke, followed immediately by a large, yellow-blue flame. It will burn for about 20 to 30 seconds and the other kids will "ooh" and "aah" the whole time.

Do not touch the tart pan, as it gets very hot. And, once again, make sure that you are in a well ventilated area.

4. When the fire has died out, hold out the hand that held the potassium permanganate and show it to everyone. No holes? Put a little glycerine on your tongue and stick it out. No mutation? Explain that it is very important to clean up messes, especially chemical ones, because you never know when chemicals are going to react with one another. In this case, if they are separate, no problem, but if you were to put your hand in your mouth ... pause for effect ...

How Come, Huh?

As the glycerine (the clear liquid) is absorbed by the potassium permanganate (the purple powder), the molecules in the powder start to react with the molecules in the liquid. As the molecules split apart, they rapidly release the energy that held them together. This heat energy is enough to create a fire. If you watch carefully, you will see that the reaction spits little bombs as it proceeds.

Poly A/B Cup Heater

The Experiment

An ounce of polyurethane A is mixed with an ounce of polyurethane B. The two liquids are stirred in a large, plastic cup and then all of a sudden ... nothing happens. So you set the mixture aside and go about your business only to find that a large cup of stiff rubbery foam starts to grow out of your cup. Polymer chemistry has the last laugh again!

Materials

1   1 oz. bottle of polyurethane A
1   1 oz. bottle of polyurethane B
1   Craft stick
1   12 oz. plastic cup
1   Pair of goggles
1   Pie tin

Procedure

1. Put your goggles on for safety. Put the plastic cup in the pie tin. Empty the contents of the 1 oz. bottle of polyurethane A into the cup. Add the contents of the second bottle, labeled polyurethane B.

2. Take the craft stick and stir the two compounds together thoroughly. You will see an amber-colored solution but not much else. Place your hands around the sides of the cup and mentally record the temperature that you feel.

POLY A

POLY B

CRAFT STICK

STIR

CUP

3. Toss the st_____ gar-
bage and set the cup where you can
observe it. We recommend you do
this in a well ventilated area and
avoid snorting this stuff directly.

4. After about 60 seconds, the
reaction begins and the two liquids
produce a gas that is trapped in a
warm, sticky liquid. This is the foam
polyurethane that is a common part
of our world. Place your hands
around the sides of the cup again and
feel for a temperature change.

5. The foam will continue to grow and spill out over the edge
of the cup. As the foam is growing and oozing out of the cup, there is
a great temptation to touch it. If you do, nothing will harm you, but
you will coat your fingers with a sticky foam that will harden quickly
and will be virtually impossible to remove.

If you can find a tall, skinny container, the foam will fill the
container and eventually harden. In either case, sticky fingers or
foamy container, you should get a big kick out of the reaction.

How Come, Huh?

The reaction between the two liquids produced a gas and a
plastic that eventually hardened. The gas bubbles got trapped in the
liquid and expanded toward the opening of the cup. The liquid was
just sticky enough to hold the gas in place. Then the liquid hardened
into a solid.

Instant Ice Pack

The Experiment

This is a great experiment that allows you to demonstrate one of the characteristics of a chemical reaction, the absorption of heat energy. This is called an endothermic reaction. It is easy to identify this kind of reaction because it is cold to the touch. In this case, ammonium nitrate (famous for being a component of fertilizer) absorbs heat from the room when it is dissolved in water. The temperature of the water can be lowered as much as 16° Fahrenheit, which also makes this a great compound for emergency cold packs.

Materials

1   1 oz. bottle of ammonium nitrate
1   Baggie
     Water
     Fingers

Procedure

1.   Open the bottle of ammonium nitrate and fill the cap with the pellets. Empty the capful of pellets into the baggie and recap your bottle.

2.   Pinch the ammonium nitrate through the baggie and feel for a temperature change. One would correctly assume at this point that there should be no noticeable difference in temperature because there is no water.

3.   Pour a small amount of room-temperature water into the baggie, enough to fill it about one-quarter full.

4. Tip the b[...]nd forth to dissolve the pellets and, at the same time, feel the sides of the baggie. You should note a significant temperature change. If you are having a tough time with this, roll the pellets between your fingers through the baggie.

5. When you are all done, either empty the contents of the bag down the drain or go find a brown spot on the lawn and fertilize the grass.

How Come, Huh?

When the water is added to the ammonium nitrate, the ions of both the ammonium and the nitrate dissolve into the water, and heat is absorbed during the breaking of the ionic bonds. This type of reaction is known as an endothermic reaction in the science world because heat is absorbed.

Another way of thinking about this is that the ammonium nitrate is dumped into the baggie. When it is just sitting there reacting with air, nothing happens. When water is added to the equation, the heat from the water is used by the ammonium nitrate to break the bonds and split the compound into two halves.

The Chemistry Behind It

$$NH_4NO_{3(s)} + H_2O_{(l)} + Heat \qquad NH_4^+{}_{(aq)} + NO_3^-{}_{(aq)}$$

Big Idea 4

Liquids that allow an electric current to pass through them are called conductors. Electricity can be used to separate compounds into elements, attach compounds to one another, and produce changes in pH. Metals can also be used to generate the flow of electricity in the presence of electrical conductors.

Le Boom du Jour • B. K. Hixson

Liquid Conductors

The Experiment

OK, we've got the solid conductors covered. We know that sparks will jump through the air, so we'll say that for the gases too. What about liquids? You always hear that you should not use electrical devices when you are in the tub, or shower and shave with an electrical shaver plugged into the wall. This lab does two things: explores conductivity of liquids and sets you up to understand electroplating.

Materials

1   Battery with holder
1   Lamp with socket
3   Alligator clips
1   250 mL beaker
    Salt, 2 tablespoons
    150 mL lemon juice
    150 mL vinegar
    Water

Procedure

1. Snap the battery into the battery holder. Bend the tabs on the ends of each clip outward so the alligator clips can be attached easily.

2. Assemble the circuit pictured at the right and make sure that the bulb lights up when everything is connected together.

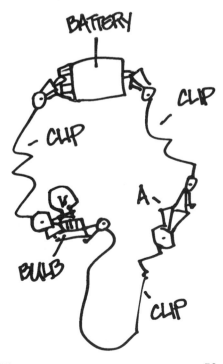

‎Liquid Conductors

3. Separate the two alligator clips (point A in the circuit) and test the conductivity of water by lowering the clips into the water. If the lightbulb lights, that means the electrons are flowing, and the liquid is a conductor. If it doesn't light, the liquid is an insulator.

4. Test each of the other three liquids, one at a time, by dipping the alligator clips into the beaker. Mark your findings in the appropriate boxes in the data table below. When you get done with our suggestions, add two liquids that you choose, and test them in the same way.

Data & Observations

Liquid	Conductor? Y/N	Insulator? Y/N
Water		
Salt Water		
Lemon Juice		
Vinegar		
A.		
B.		

How Come, Huh?

What you should have found is that water is actually not a very good conductor. However, if a liquid has an acid in it, such as vinegar (acetic acid) or lemon juice (citric acid), or if it contains something like salt that dissolves into a solution and produces ions (charged particles), it is a good conductor.

Water is a bipolar molecule, meaning that it has a positive charge on one end and a negative charge on the other, but is not charged itself. It is neutral, or balanced. These other liquids you tested have electrical charges, and this allows them to collect and pass electrons along through them with ease.

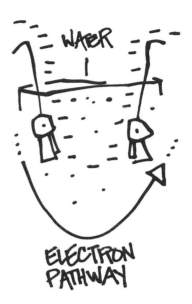

Science Fair Extensions

1. With adult supervision and permission, collect several acids and bases. Test each of them with your conductivity tester to see if some work better than others.

2. Find out what kinds of chemicals you can add to water to enhance its conductivity and promote the movement of ions and other charged particles through it.

Exploding Water

The Experiment

Electricity can also be used to manufacture products. In this case, we are going to introduce you to a process called hydrolysis, which uses electricity to split water molecules into hydrogen and oxygen gases. Both of these gases are sold commercially and have different characteristics that you will explore in this lab.

Materials

2 Alligator clip jumper wires
1 Bare copper wire
1 D battery holder
1 D battery
1 1 oz. bottle of phenolphthalein
    in ethyl alcohol
1 9 oz. clear plastic cup
1 Insulated copper wire
1 1 oz. bottle of sodium sulfate
1 Plastic test tube
1 Craft stick
1 Book of matches
Adult Supervision

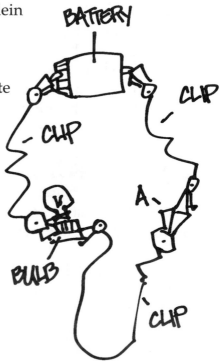

Procedure

1. Insert the D battery in the battery holder. Connect one alligator clip to each battery terminal and set this apparatus aside.

2. Fill the 9 oz. plastic cup with water and add one capful of the phenolphthalein. Now add one capful of sodium sulfate powder to the mixture and stir the contents of the cup with the craft stick until all of the powder has dissolved.

3. Fill the plastic test tube with the solution you've just made. Place your thumb over the top of the test tube, turn it upside down, and place it in the cup. Lean the test tube up against the wall of the cup and locate the insulated wire. It should have two bare, exposed ends.

4. Slide the insulated wire underneath the mouth of the test tube so that one end of the wire is at least halfway into the tube, but still submerged. Drape the remaining wire over the top of the cup so it can be connected to the battery later.

5. Place one end of the bare copper wire in the solution. Drape the remainder of the wire over the side so that it can also be connected to the battery. Use the illustration above as a guide.

6. Using the alligator clips, connect the insulated wire to the negative side of the battery, and connect the bare copper wire to the positive terminal. Observe the color changes that take place inside the test tube as the electricity starts to flow.

Exploding Water

7. Allow the gas to collect inside the tube for a few minutes; then carefully lift the tube up, keeping it upside down. When an adult comes to your lab area, place your thumb over the end of the tube and flip the tube right side up. Ask the adult to light a match and bring it near the edge of the test tube. When the match gets close, quickly remove your thumb and watch the reaction.

How Come, Huh?

Water is composed of 2 parts hydrogen hooked to 1 part oxygen. As a general rule, the atoms stay hooked together until something produces enough energy to split them apart. In this case, the electricity is the energy that splits the atoms.

Hydrogen is flammable. It also has a positive charge. That means that if hydrogen gas is produced when an electric current travels through water, the hydrogen will collect at the negative terminal of the current. When the match was brought near the hydrogen gas, it ignited and burned rapidly, expanding and creating a "whoop" when the air rushed out of the tube.

The pink color was produced by phenolphthalein, an acid/base indicator. As the reaction proceeded, the pH of the solution changed, and this resulted in the color change.

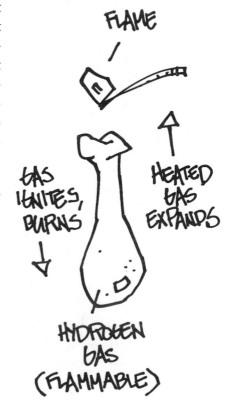

FLAME

GAS IGNITES, BURNS

HEATED GAS EXPANDS

HYDROGEN GAS (FLAMMABLE)

Copper Coated Clips

The Experiment

Electricity can flow through certain liquids. Its ability to do this allows it to be used to coat objects with metal. This coating process is called electroplating and is used extensively in industry for all kinds of applications—from making jewelry, to coating machine parts to prevent corrosion, to applying thin magnetic coats to speakers to make them perform more efficiently. In this lab, we are going to coat a paper clip with copper.

Materials

1   D battery with holder
1   Lamp with socket
3   Alligator clips
1   250 mL beaker
1   1 oz. bottle of copper sulfate solution
1   Tablespoon
1   Paper clip
1   Nail, 8 penny
1   Craft stick
1   Strip of fabric, 1 inch x 4 inches
1   Glass microscope slide
1   Plastic straw
    Water

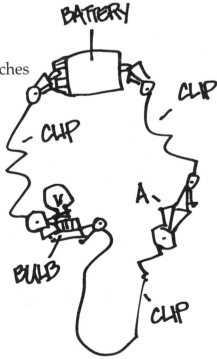

Procedure

1. Snap the battery into the battery holder. Bend out the tabs on the alligator clips so that they can be attached easily.

2. Assemble the circuit that is pictured at the right, and make sure that the bulb lights up when everything is connected.

Copper Coated Clips

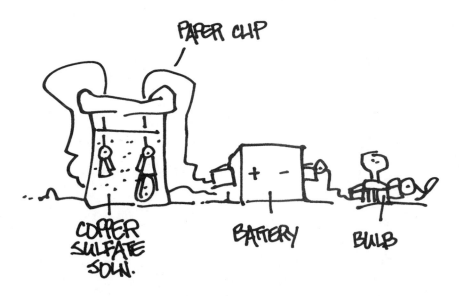

PAPER CLIP

COPPER SULFATE SOLN.

BATTERY

BULB

3. Fill the 250 mL beaker with water and add a tablespoon of copper sulfate. Stir. If all the copper sulfate dissolves, keep adding more until there is a small quantity at the bottom of the beaker.

4. Separate the two alligator clips (point A in the circuit) and clip the paper clip onto the negative terminal. Check the battery to see which terminal is negative. Lower the paper clip on one side of the beaker and the other alligator clip on the other side. Wait about 3 minutes.

5. When time is up, pull the paper clip up out of the solution and take a peek at the deposit that is coating the wire.

6. Look at the list of materials in the data table on the next page and make a prediction—yes or no—about whether or not the item will take a copper coat. Write your prediction for each. Then, test all the materials that are listed and see how accurate your predictions are. Record your observations in the data table.

Data & Observations

Item	Prediction	Coating? Y/N
Nail		
Craft Stick		
Fabric		
Microscope Slide		
Plastic Straw		

How Come, Huh?

What you should have discovered is that metal objects make excellent conductors. Of all the materials you tested, they are the only ones that can be coated with the copper ions.

When you added the copper sulfate, it dissolved and broke into charged particles called ions. The copper ions had a positive charge and the sulfate ions had a negative charge. When the two alligator clips were dipped into the solution, one had a positive charge and the other had a negative charge. The negatively charged alligator clip, holding the paper clip, attracted the positively charged copper ions that produced that brownish, gooey coating that you saw on the paper clip.

Science Fair Extensions

3. Find out what other kinds of metals will dissolve in solution and how those metals can be applied to objects made of different materials.

Hand Battery

The Experiment

You are going to generate an electric current that you are actually a part of by placing both hands on two dissimilar metals.

Materials

1   DC microammeter
    (100 microamps)
1   Aluminum plate, 6 inches by 6
       inches
1   Copper plate, 6 inches by 6 inches
1   Lead plate, 6 inches by 6 inches
1   Zinc plate, 6 inches by 6 inches
2   Alligator clips
1   Towel

Procedure

1. Place the aluminum and copper plates on a non-metallic surface.

2. Using the alligator clips, connect one plate to one of the microammeter's terminals and the other plate to the other terminal. Use the illustration at the right as a guide.

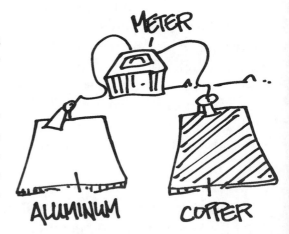

3. Place both hands on the plates and leave them there for 30 seconds. Check the reading on the microammeter over time. If you are having difficulty getting a reading, rinse your hands under warm water, blot them on a towel so that they are damp but not wet, and place them on the plates again.

4. Try the different combinations of metal plates suggested in the data table below. Place your hands on the combinations of metals and wait about 30 seconds to take a reading.

Data & Observations

Plates	Ammeter Reading
Aluminum/Copper	
Aluminum/Lead	
Aluminum/Zinc	
Copper/Lead	
Copper/Zinc	
Lead/Zinc	

How Come, Huh?

When you touch the two plates, electrons flow from the copper plate into your hand. This leaves the copper plate with a positive charge. On the other plate, the opposite reaction occurs. The aluminum grabs electrons from your hand and accumulates a negative charge. So, you have electrons flowing from the copper plate into one hand, through your body, and out the other hand into the aluminum plate.

From the aluminum plate, the excess electrons flow into the microammeter on their way to the copper plate. Depending on the combination of metals, you will get a variety of readings. The success you have using various metals will depend on each metal's electric potential, which is its ability to gain or lose electrons—the greater the difference between the two metals, the higher the voltage.

Hand Battery

As an aside, the moisture produced by your hands acts like the battery acid in a battery. It lowers the resistance so that the electrons can move freely across the surface of the skin. If the air is really dry, wetting your hands provides the necessary moisture.

ELECTRON FLOW

Science Fair Extensions

4. Repeat the experiment with other kinds of metals and see which one works best to produce the greatest potential.

5. With the supervision of an adult, dissect a battery and examine the metals and electrolytes that are used.

Because most batteries are made using strong acids or alkaline substances, you will want to wear goggles and gloves while you are examining these items.

Lemons in Series

The Experiment

Lemons make you pucker when you bite into them. This is due, in part, to the citric acid that lemons and other fruits, such as oranges, grapefruits, and kiwis all have.

If you think back to your liquid conductors lab, you will remember that water that had a little acid added to it was much more efficient at conducting electricity than just plain water. We are going to take it one more step with this lab. Not only are we going to conduct electricity, but we are also going to make a battery that *produces* electricity using a lemon. What will those citrus growers think of next?

Materials

2   Lemons
1   Knife
4   Alligator clips
3   Zinc strips, 0.25 inch by 4 inches
3   Copper strips, 0.25 inch by 4 inches
1   Light-emitting diode (LED)
    Adult Supervision/Assistance

Procedure

1.   You will want to get ripe, juicy lemons for this lab—the juicier, the better. Take the two lemons and firmly roll them on the table to break the inner tissue, but not the skin.

2.   Have an adult help you cut both lemons in half. Set two of the cut lemon halves aside.

Lemons in Series

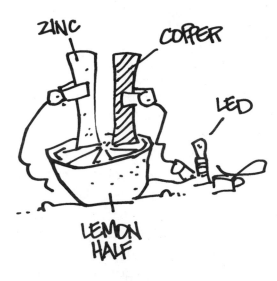

ZINC
COPPER
LED
LEMON HALF

3. Insert a copper and zinc strip into the fleshy part of one lemon half. Avoid the white, pulpy rind. Attach an alligator clip to each strip.

4. When you look at the LED, you will notice that one wire is longer than the other. Connect the longer of the two wires to the alligator lead coming from the copper strip. Attach the shorter wire to the lead coming from the zinc strip. Check to see if any light is being produced.

5. Insert zinc and copper strips into the two other lemon halves. Using the diagram below, hook two and then three of the lemon halves in series. Be sure to always attach zinc to copper electrodes. See if the LED lights each time. Record your observations in the data table on the next page.

ZINC
COPPER
LEMONS
LED

Le Boom du Jour • *B. K. Hixson*

Data & Observations

Lemon Halves	LED Light Up? Y/N
Single	
Double	
Triple	

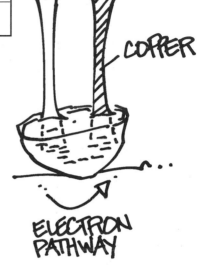

ZINC

COPPER

ELECTRON PATHWAY

How Come, Huh?

The juice in the lemons contains citric acid, which is a weak acid and which also is what is called an electrolyte—a solution that conducts electricity.

The zinc strip gives up electrons more easily than the copper strip, so when everything is hooked up in series, the electrons leave the zinc, zip through the lemon juice, and the lemon juice gives the electrons a push into the copper strip. The number of electrons—voltage—is too few to light up the diode. When you hook three batteries in series, as you saw in the previous lab, the voltage increases. With three lemon halves, there is enough to make the LED glow.

Science Fair Extensions

6. Repeat the experiment with other citrus fruits and see what works best as a battery. You can buy voltmeters that are very sensitive and actually measure the voltage produced by lemons, oranges, grapefruits, and other citrus fruits.

Electric Potato Pie

The Experiment

We have electrocuted lemons, chased electrons through vinegar, produced sound, light, heat, and magnetic effects, and even coated metals with metals using electricity. Why not run some juice through a potato to see what happens?

Materials

1   Potato, large and fresh
1   Knife
2   Bell wires, insulated, each 4 inches long
1   Pair of wire strippers
2   Alligator clips
1   Transistor battery, 9v
Adult Supervision

Procedure

1.   Carefully cut the potato in half with the knife.

2.   Using the wire strippers, remove the plastic coating from both ends of each piece of the bell wire.

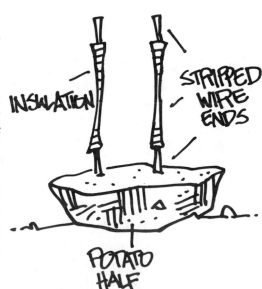

3.   Insert the stripped ends of the wires into the potato, spacing them about 1.5 inches apart. Use the illustration at the right as a guide.

4.   Attach one alligator clip to the end of each wire that is sticking out of the potato. Connect the free ends of the alligator clips to the 9v battery.

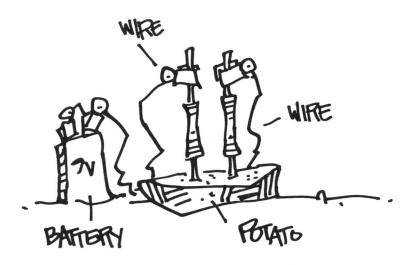

WIRE

WIRE

BATTERY

POTATO

You will notice that there is a reaction at the end of each terminal. Take a peek and record what you see in the data table below.

Data & Observations

Terminal	Reaction
Positive	
Negative	

How Come, Huh?

The electrons flowing through the potato caused a reaction at both terminals. The negative terminal produced hydrogen bubbles where the electricity caused the water in the potato to separate into hydrogen and oxygen. The positive terminal turned green where copper ions from the wire migrated out into the potato tissue.

Science Fair Extensions

7. Try other roots. Yams, sweet potatoes, turnips, radishes, carrots, and onions, among others, are all likely candidates for experimentation.

Big Idea 5

Compounds and elements can combine or bond with one another in groups of two or more. When this happens, a new compound is formed that has its own, unique set of characteristics and can be identified by a change of state, change of color, odor produced, light produced, or heat gain or loss.

Magnesium Floodlamps

The Experiment

Chemicals are notorious for storing energy. TNT, dynamite, and a host of other explosives have been used to store and then release, at a very specific moment, energy. In addition to explosions, chemicals are also very good at releasing light energy that is stored in their chemical bonds. Magnesium is one element that is used extensively in fireworks for this very purpose. It also makes a great fire starter.

Materials

1   Propane torch or Bunsen burner
1   Ignitor or book of matches
1   Pair of test tube holders
1   4 inch strip of magnesium ribbon
    Adult Supervision

Procedure

1. You do not need to wear a welding helmet or even protective eyewear for this experiment, but the light that is produced is VERY BRIGHT.

2. Tear off a 4 inch piece of magnesium ribbon and clip it into the test tube holder. Light the torch and hold the magnesium in the flame. It will take a couple of seconds, but you will see a very bright, white light once the magnesium reaches its kindling point.

How Come, Huh?

The heat from the flame excites the magnesium atoms, which start to bounce around. When they get moving too fast, they rip apart, releasing the chemical energy stored in the bonds as light and heat— 5000° Celsius, to be exact.

Instant Sunshine

The Experiment
If there is a change of color, that is a pretty good clue that a chemical reaction has taken place. This experiment illustrates that concept for you. Keep in mind that there may be more than one clue that there has been a reaction or change. In this experiment, two clear liquids are mixed together to produce a bright yellow solid.

Materials
2   Test tubes
1   Bottle of lead nitrate solution
1   Bottle of potassium iodide solution
1   Pair of rubber gloves

LEAD NITRATE

POTASSIUM IODIDE

TEST TUBE

Procedure
1. Before you mix chemicals, you should always put goggles on your peepers and rubber gloves on your hands. **Lead can be absorbed through the skin; be careful.**

2. Fill one test tube with a half an inch of lead nitrate solution. Observe the color. Fill the other test tube with the same amount of potassium iodide and note that color. Record the colors in the data table on the next page.

3. Mix the two test tubes together. Congratulations. Your solution has crashed. If you allow the tube to sit for a minute or two, the solid will settle to the bottom of the tube and a clear liquid will appear just above it. These are two new chemicals. The bright yellow solid is a precipitate called lead iodide. The liquid is potassium nitrate.

4. Lead is a very poisonous compound that can accumulate in your body over time. Be very careful with this chemical. When you are ready to dispose of it, pour it into a napkin, wrap it up, seal it in a baggie, and place it in the trash.

Data & Observations

Chemical	Color
Lead Nitrate	
Potassium Iodide	
Lead Iodide	
Potassium Nitrate	

How Come, Huh?

When chemicals react with one another to form new compounds, they take on different shapes. This means that they can also absorb and reflect different colors of light.

As the lead nitrate and potassium iodide (both colorless) react, they produce lead iodide (bright yellow solid) and potassium nitrate (clear liquid). When lead iodide is formed, the shape of the chemical reflects the yellow color that you see.

Coffee Capers

The Experiment

It's just a fact that some places in the world do not have clean water. There are all sorts of little critters zipping around in the streams, rivers, and lakes that are just dying to take up residence in your gastrointestinal tract and make life one mad dash. To cure this problem, folks who work and live in developing countries add potassium permanganate to the water supplies to kill bacteria, fungi, and other critters.

We are going to use it to demonstrate a different idea—how compounds change color when you start stealing electrons and changing their shape.

Materials

1   1 oz. bottle of dilute sodium hydroxide
1   Bottle of potassium permanganate
1   Test tube
1   1 mL pipette
1   Paper towel
1   Pair of rubber gloves
    Water

Procedure

1. Wear gloves. The potassium permanganate should not come in contact with your skin. Add a pinch of potassium permanganate to the bottom of the empty test tube—maybe enough powder to equal half a pea. Fill the test tube three-quarters full of cold water. When the water hits the potassium permanganate, it will immediately dissolve the powder and produce a beautiful, deep-purple color.

2. Carefully remove the cap from the bottle of sodium hydroxide and add two pipettefuls to the test tube that has the potassium permanganate solution in it. Sodium hydoxide is a very strong base and this raises the pH of the solution considerably.

3. Roll the paper towel into a tube and slide the end of it into the purple solution. Gently remove the paper towel and take note of the three distinct colors that you will see. Then toss the paper towel in the trash and rinse the remainder of the solution down the drain with some water.

How Come, Huh?

The purple color in the potassium permanganate is produced by the manganese ion. Manganese has a 7+ charge, or oxidation state (Mn^{7+}). This means that we have stolen 7 electrons from the atom, which does not make the atom happy. In fact, it will be looking around for places to steal some of the electrons back.

When the manganese atom steals electrons, it changes the shape of the atom, which in turn changes the color that we see with our eyes. If it steals 1 electron, making it a 6+ oxidation state, the purple liquid appears to turn green. If it steals 2 more electrons, making it a 4+ oxidation state, the greenish liquid appears to turn brown.

Acid Digestion

The Experiment

Acids and metals have never gotten along very well. We are going to take advantage of that fact in this experiment. Dilute sulfuric acid is added to mossy zinc. When the two react, they produce a flammable gas … and an odor that rivals any of the worst.

Materials

1   20 mm by 150 mm test tube
1   1 oz. bottle of 1M sulfuric acid
3   Mossy zinc pieces
1   Book of matches
1   Pair of goggles
    Water
    Adult Supervision

SULFURIC ACID

MOSSY ZINC

TEST TUBE

Procedure

1. Add enough sulfuric acid to a test tube to fill it about 2 inches. Drop a couple of pieces of mossy zinc into the acid and observe what happens.

2. After the reaction has proceeded for about 30 seconds, darken the room. Ask an adult to carefully light a match and hold it near the mouth of the tube. If you look closely, you will see a bright blue flame ignite the gasses at the top of the tube and migrate to the liquid layer. When the flame gets to the liquid layer, the tube will produce a small "whoop."

3. This reaction will continue for several minutes. Be sure to let the tube have time to recharge (fill with gas). Have an adult relight the tube as many times as is possible.

4. Turn the lights back on and gently waft the odor that is produced by the reaction. Never stick your nose directly over the tube and snort the gases into your nasal passages.

How Come, Huh?

The acid reacts with the zinc to produce hydrogen sulfide—rotten egg gas. This explains the smell. The hydrogen is flammable, so when the match is introduced into the mouth of the tube, it ignites the gas. The "whoop" was caused by the rushing of hot gas out of the tube, which produced a vibration at the top of the tube when it escaped. Sound being produced by rapidly expanding air, take 3…

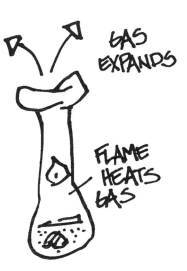

GAS EXPANDS

FLAME HEATS GAS

Science Fair Extensions

8. Perform the experiments in tubes of different diameters and lengths. You will find that both the diameter of the tube and the distance between the top of the tube and the liquid level factor into the sound that is produced.

9. Any rapidly burning gas confined to a small space will produce a sound as it is escaping. With the permission of your parents, research other flammable gases and explore the possibilities for making noise.

Rotten Egg Gas

The Experiment

Volcanos, gas wells, coal pits, sulfur springs, and the gastrointestinal exit ports of individuals who have eaten large quantities of fried onion rings all have one thing in common. They produce hydrogen sulfide gas.

In this experiment, you will be generating hydrogen sulfide gas by mixing a base with an acid in a cup. The base is a mixture of calcium sulfide and sodium bicarbonate, and the acid is plain, old vinegar. This is definitely a face wrinkler and should be shared only with a close friend or cherished sibling.

Materials

1   1 oz. bottle of acetic acid
1   Vial of calcium sulfide with sodium bicarbonate
1   Plastic salsa cup, 2 oz.

Procedure

1. Open one vial of calcium sulfide mixture and pour its entire contents into the salsa cup. Dispose of the vial.

2. Set the cup down and remove the cap from the acetic acid.

3. Pour one-quarter of the bottle of acetic acid into the cup and step back. The acetic acid will immediately react with the powder in the cup and produce a large quantity of foam. All the cool fizzing is produced by the rotten egg gas and carbon dioxide that are being released from the solution.

4. After the reaction occurs, rinse out the paper cup and toss it into the garbage can.

5. In high concentrations, the hydrogen sulfide gas can be poisonous and **should not be directly inhaled from the cup. You should not perform this experiment and hold it directly under the nose of anyone.**

How Come, Huh?

Sulfur compounds are characteristically foul smelling, and hydrogen sulfide is no exception. In fact, one of these stinky little buggers can be smelled by itself even if it is mixed in with as many as fifty million other molecules that are of the non-stinky variety.

When calcium sulfide reacts with acetic acid (vinegar), it forms hydrogen sulfide and calcium acetate, while the sodium bicarbonate produces carbon dioxide and sodium acetate when vinegar is added.

The carbon dioxide gas prevents a large buildup of hydrogen sulfide molecules in the cup and helps carry the hydrogen sulfide gas out of the cup.

The Chemistry Behind It

The calcium sulfide reacts with the vinegar. This produces hydrogen sulfide gas, the stinky stuff, and residual calcium doo doo. Not the official term, but you get the idea.

$$CaS \ (s) + 2CH_3COOH \ (l) \rightarrow H_2S \ (g) + Ca(CH_3COO)_2 \ (aq)$$

Flame Jumper

The Experiment

Light a candle and let it burn for a while on the lab table. Blow out the candle. Hold a match a few centimeters above the wick and watch the flame jump from the match back down to the wick without ever touching the wick itself. Mission accomplished!

Materials

1   Candle
1   Book of matches
Adult Supervision

Procedure

1.   Review the fire safety rules on page 17. This is important any time you or your friends are working with an open flame.

2.   Have an adult light a candle. Let it burn for a few minutes until some of the wax around the wick has melted.

3.   Extinguish the candle flame by licking your thumb and forefinger and then pinching the flame out. Try not to disturb or disperse the smoke by blowing the flame out.

4.   Have an adult relight the candle by holding a match a few centimeters above the wick, directly in the smoke coming from the flame. The flame will jump from the match to the wick.

How Come, Huh?

The smoke rising from the wick is made primarily of vaporized wax. This is the gas state of the wax and it is highly flammable. When you hold the match above the wick, this wax vapor is very near the kindling point of wax and catches on fire easily. Once the gas has been ignited, it will quickly ignite the rest of the vapor coming from the wick and reignite the wick itself.

It appears that the flame jumps from the match to the wick. In reality, the flame from the match is lighting the wax vapor on fire—which almost instantly ignites the wick.

The other thing worth noting is that you have all three phases of wax present in this experiment. The solid wax is quite evident, as is the gas state (the smoke). If you look carefully at the base of the wick, there is also a small pool of liquid wax.

Science Fair Extensions

10. Does the size of the candle affect the distance the flame will jump? Try using a large candle and a small one. Burn the candles for the same amount of time; then with adult supervision, of course, put out the flame.

11. Birthday candles are great for experiments. Try this one with adult supervision. Does the color of the candle affect its burning time? Set candles in small holders of play dough. Light 4 different colors at the same time and chart minutes until the candles burn out. Repeat at least 3 times, record your data, and write your conclusions.

Burning Steel

The Experiment

In this experiment, you will be equipped with goggles and fire safety information. Armed with this information, attempt to melt a large steel nail over a very small flame in your desire to understand what the heck a kindling point is.

After a few attempts (you judge if you are successful or not), another type of steel (steel wool) will be placed into the flame. This is the wool of a lamb that has been living near a hard-hat construction area all of its life (just kidding). You will hold a piece of the steel wool (not the entire lamb) over the flame and observe that it will indeed reach the kindling point very quickly and send out a shower of golden sparkles in celebration.

Materials

1   Pair of goggles
1   Candle, votive
1   Pie tin
1   Book of matches
1   Test tube holder
1   #16 Nail
1   00000 Steel wool pad (without soap on it)
1   Fire blanket / fire extinguisher
    Adult Supervision

Procedure

1. Put goggles on and place the candle in the center of the pie tin. Ask an adult to light the candle.

2. With an adult watching, place the nail in the test tube holder and insert the nail into the flame of the candle. Use the illustration above as a guide. Roll the nail around inside the flame of the candle and do your very best to get it to catch on fire. After 30 seconds or so, place the HOT nail inside the pie tin. **Do NOT touch it!**

3.	Take the piece of steel wool and "tease" (pull apart) the fibers into a large ball to expose the steel to plenty of oxygen—the bigger, the better. Clip one side of the ball of steel wool into the test tube holder and then place the steel wool ball in the candle flame. Use the illustration at the right as a guide.

4.	The steel wool will ignite, burn, and smoke. Be sure to keep holding the burning steel wool over the pie tin. When the reaction is done, release the wool from the clip and place it in the pie tin. When everything has cooled off, throw away the burned remains and keep the nail.

Data & Observations

Circle the word that best answers the question asked.

1.	Which material, steel wool or the nail, had a greater surface area exposed to the flame?

Steel Wool 		*Nail*

2.	Which material, steel wool or the nail, was surrounded by more oxygen?

Steel Wool 		*Nail*

Burning Steel

How Come, Huh?

This is strictly a matter of surface area. The nail will get hot but will not burn. Its mass is too large and it conducts the heat away from the flame. The steel wool is extremely fine, on the other hand, and has lots of oxygen between the fibers to help it ignite. The steel wool will reach the kindling point (the temperature when a substance bursts into flames). Did you know that the temperature at which iron catches on fire (the kindling point) is actually lower than the kindling point for paper? The trick is getting enough oxygen to a large enough surface area for the reaction to keep going.

Science Fair Extensions

12. You may want to experiment with different grades of steel wool. It comes in various thicknesses, ranging from 00000, which is very fine, to 5, which is not. Make sure you do not get the kind that has soap in it.

13. Try dipping the steel wool in various liquids, allowing it to dry, and then placing it in the flame. Liquids? Cola, water, juice, alcohol, soap, and so on. Use a stopwatch to record the amount of time before the wool catches on fire each time. Be sure to have an adult nearby.

Orange Sorbet

The Experiment

Baking soda and aluminum sulfate (the pickling spice alum) are mixed together with a little soap. The result is a huge pile of orange bubbles that look like a creamy, orange dessert.

Materials

1   Pair of goggles
1   Pair of gloves
1   Vial of aluminum sulfate powder
1   Vial of sodium bicarbonate powder
1   1 oz. bottle of detergent with squirt cap
1   1 oz. bottle of red food coloring
1   1 oz. bottle of yellow food coloring
1   Toobe, 8 inches high with round, plastic base
1   Preform tube
1   #3 Solid stopper
     Water

Procedure

1.   Fill the Toobe one-third full with water, add a capful of baking soda powder, add several drops of yellow food coloring, cover with the palm of your hand, and shake like crazy. Place the Toobe in the center of the pie tin.

Orange Sorbet

2. Add 2 ounces of water to the preform tube. Then add one cap of aluminum sulfate powder, one dash of detergent, and a couple of squirts of red food coloring. Stopper the preform tube and shake like crazy to mix the contents.

3. Quickly pour the aluminum sulfate solution into the Toobe and observe what happens.

4. A pile of orange foam will rise quickly up out of the Toobe and spill all over the table. Feign disgust, shock, disbelief, or any other contortion that works.

How Come, Huh?

When you mix baking soda and aluminum sulfate in solution, they react with each other and release a gas called carbon dioxide. The gas forms a bubble and escapes to the top of the solution. The soap strengthens the solution and allows gas to be trapped.

As the reaction proceeds, more and more bubbles are produced, and the bubbles push those bubbles ahead of them out of the way and onto the table. The soap allows the bubbles to persist and the result is a big pile of bubbles that looks like orange sorbet.

ALUMINUM SULFATE

SODIUM BICARBONATE

TOOBE IN PIE TIN

Limewater Precipitation

The Experiment

The nickname for calcium hydroxide is limewater. Calcium hydroxide (called lime) is used to manufacture cement. Limewater is a strong base, has a very nasty taste, and **should never be ingested**.

We are going to use limewater to create a chemical reaction with your breath. When you breathe out, your body gets rid of carbon dioxide. If this carbon dioxide comes in contact with the calcium hydroxide, which is a clear solution, it reacts and produces a new chemical called calcium carbonate. This new chemical is insoluble in water and produces a milky white solution. What more could you want in a chemical change?

Materials

STRAW

CALCIUM HYDROXIDE

BAGGIE

1   Bottle of limewater
1   Baggie, ziplock
1   Straw

Procedure

1. Open the bottle of limewater and pour half the contents, or about one ounce, into the baggie. Observe the characteristics of this compound. Is it clear, colored, transparent, translucent, or opaque? Does it have a distinctive odor?

2. When you are done with your observations, slide the straw into the baggie and wrap the baggie around the straw to prevent any liquid from bubbling out while you blow.

Limewater Precipitation

3. Take a deep breath and gently blow into the solution in the baggie, making lots of bubbles. Observe the solution as you blow, and note any changes in color, transparency, or temperature.

4. Continue to blow into the baggie until the liquid turns a milky white color, like skim milk.

5. When you are done with the experiment, you can wash the contents of the bag down the drain with plenty of water and toss the baggie into the garbage. Be sure to wash your hands when you are done with this lab.

How Come, Huh?

The carbon dioxide in your breath bubbled up through the calcium hydroxide solution. When the two chemicals came in contact with each other, calcium carbonate was produced. This is a white solid that does not dissolve in water. Because the particles that were formed were so small, they stayed suspended in the solution and reflected the light from the room back to your eyes.

Big Idea 6

The number of free ions in a solution is measured on a scale from 1 to 14, called the pH scale. A solution that tests at 7 is considered neutral, a solution below 7 is acidic, and a solution above 7 is basic. Specially prepared papers have been created to identify acids, bases, and degrees of pH.

The Litmus Test

The Experiment

To introduce the idea of acids and bases, we are going to start big and work down to the specific. Litmus paper is handy stuff that comes in two colors, red and blue. Each color identifies a specific group of compounds. Red litmus paper turns blue in the presence of a base, and blue litmus paper turns red in the presence of an acid. These papers do not tell you the degree to which a liquid is an acid or a base. They simply tell that the liquid is an acid or base. We will get more specific in the next couple of labs.

Materials

1	Vial of red litmus paper
1	Vial of blue litmus paper
1	Bottle of ammonia
1	Bottle of vinegar
1	Bottle of sodium hydroxide
1	Bottle of sulfuric acid, dilute
5	Pipettes
5	Paper towels
	Water

Procedure

1. Place one piece of red and one piece of blue litmus paper on a paper towel.

2. Open the bottle of ammonia and, using a clean pipette, draw one mL of liquid up into the dispenser. Put one drop of ammonia on the red litmus paper and one drop on the blue. Observe any changes that may occur and record them in the data table on the next page. Throw the paper into the garbage after each test.

3. Repeat this procedure for the remaining four liquids. If a liquid does not cause a paper to change color, write the word "neither" in the *Acid/Base?* box.

Data & Observations

In the data table below, record any changes that occur when the liquids are placed on the pieces of litmus paper. If the blue paper remains blue, just write "blue." If it changes to red, write "red." Same with the red paper… just write the color it ends up as.

Liquid Tested	Blue Litmus	Red Litmus	Acid/Base?
Ammonia			
Vinegar			
Sodium Hydroxide			
Sulfuric Acid			
Water			

How Come, Huh?

The paper is treated with a chemical called an acid base indicator. This chemical responds to acids and bases by changing its shape, just a little bit, in the presence of the chemicals. This change in shape affects the way that the indicator absorbs and reflects light. Paper that was once reflecting red light will now absorb that color and reflect blue, and vice-versa. If there are no color changes, the liquid that you are testing is probably neutral.

pH Paper

The Experiment

OK, we've grouped some chemicals into acids and bases. This is kind of like separating vegetables and fruits. It is a start, but what if we want to get more specific?

The pH scale was devised not only to allow chemists to test and classify compounds as acids and bases, but also to classify the degree to which they are acidic or basic. The scale runs from 1 to 14. 7 is a neutral compound and anything below 7 is considered an acid. The lower the number, the stronger the acid is. Any chemical that tests above 7 is considered a base, and the higher the number, the stronger the base.

This lab is going to introduce you to pH paper. It is a specially treated paper that changes color in the presence of acids and bases. Using this paper, you can tell if you have an acid or a base and can determine how strong or weak it is.

Materials

1 Vial of pH paper
1 pH color key
1 Bottle of ammonia
1 Bottle of vinegar
1 Bottle of sodium hydroxide
1 Bottle of sulfuric acid, dilute
5 Pipettes
5 Paper Towels
   Water

Procedure

1. Place a piece of pH paper on a paper towel and open the bottle of ammonia. Using a clean pipette, draw one mL of liquid up into the dispenser. Put one drop of ammonia on the pH paper.

2.   When the liquid hits the paper, the paper will immediately change color. Compare the color that you see on the pH paper to the color key that is on the vial. Find the color that most closely matches the color you see and record that color's number in the data table below. Then record the meaning of that number by noting whether the liquid is an acid or base, or whether it's neutral.

3.   Repeat this procedure for the remaining four liquids. Identify each liquid as an acid, base, or neutral compound.

Data & Observations

Liquid Tested	Color Produced/ Number on pH Scale	Acid/Base/ Neutral?
Ammonia		
Vinegar		
Sodium Hydroxide		
Sulfuric Acid		
Water		

How Come, Huh?

Like the litmus paper in the previous lab, this paper is also treated with an acid base indicator. This chemical responds to acids and bases by changing its shape in the presence of other chemicals. This change in shape affects the way that the indicator absorbs and reflects light and produces the different colors that you see.

Red Cabbage to Green

The Experiment

For those of you who prefer your chemistry on a more organic level, we have a pH indicator that can be made from ordinary, right-out-of-the-grocery-bin, red cabbage. When the juice from red cabbage, which is pink, comes in contact with a strong base, like ammonia or sodium hydroxide, it changes color dramatically. But why believe us? Try it yourself.

Materials

1   Red cabbage leaf
1   Kitchen knife
4   20 mm x 150 mm test tubes
1   Test tube holder
1   Votive candle
1   Book of matches
1   Pair of goggles
1   Bottle of ammonia
1   Bottle of sodium hydroxide
1   Bottle of vinegar
1   Pipette
     Water
     Adult Supervision

Procedure

1. Using the kitchen knife, chop the red cabbage into very small pieces. The smaller that you make the pieces, the more surface there will be to react with the water and the more heat there will be to extract the indicator.

2. Fill one of the test tubes half full with chopped cabbage leaves and add water until you just cover the top of the leaf pile.

3. Put your goggles on, light the candle, clamp the tube in the holder, and heat the bottom of the test tube in the candle flame.

4. Heat the leaves until the water turns a deep purplish-red color. Remove the test tube from the flame, which you can now extinguish, and pour equal amounts of the red liquid into each of the three empty test tubes.

5. Using your pipette, add a squirt of ammonia to one tube, clean the pipette in water, add a squirt of sodium hydroxide to the second tube, clean the pipette, and add vinegar to the third tube. Observe what happens to the color of the liquid.

Data & Observations

Note the color produced when each liquid is tested with the red cabbage juice. From the color, determine if the liquid is an acid or a base.

Liquid Tested	Color Produced	Acid/Base?
Ammonia		
Sodium Hydroxide		
Vinegar		

Red Cabbage to Green

How Come, Huh?

Indicators are extremely large, complex molecules. By adding a base to the red cabbage juice indicator, you were raising the pH of the solution, and a ton of hydrogen ions were lost. When this happened, it changed the shape of the molecules.

When you change the shape of a molecule, you can also change the way that molecule captures and reflects light. In this case, the original shape of the red cabbage molecules reflected reds and purples with a couple of blues thrown in. When the hydrogen ions went on vacation, the molecules contorted into different shapes and instead of reflecting reds and purples, they reflected yellows, greens, and a blue or two.

Science Fair Extensions

14. Try adding a little vinegar to one of the two tubes that has the base (ammonia or sodium hydroxide) in it, and see if you can get the color to reverse itself from green to red.

15. Do a little reading and see if there are any other vegetables that produce indicators. Because they are in the cabbage family, you might try brussels sprouts and maybe red leaf lettuce. Squash and pumpkin skins may also provide some interesting results.

16. Test the pH of the cabbage with pH paper, before and after, to see if the results match up with those from the previous experiments.

pH Pandemonium

The Experiment

A blue chemical indicator called bromothymol blue is added to a large Toobe with water in it. A piece of dry ice (solid carbon dioxide) is added to the Toobe. When the ice hits the water, you immediately start to see the gas sublimating off the surface. It produces bubbles that rise to the surface, condense the warm air, and produce fog.

All the while that this is happening, the liquid in the Toobe turns from blue to sea-green to a light yellow color in a matter of seconds. When the reaction has proceeded to the yellow phase, you add a couple of drops of dilute sodium hydroxide, and the whole mess turns back to blue and starts over again.

Materials

2   Toobes
1   Stopper, solid, #12
1   Bottle of bromothymol blue
1   Bottle of sodium hydroxide, 10% solution
1   Bottle of vinegar
1   Pipette
1   Piece of dry ice, 2 oz. to 4 oz.
    Water
    Adult Supervision

Procedure

1. Fill the Toobe three-fourths full with water. Drop a Ping-Pong-ball-sized chunk of dry ice into the Toobe. It will immediately begin producing white bubbles that rise to the surface of the water and burst into fog.

pH Pandemonium

2. Observe this for about a minute. Not only is it entertaining, but you are acidifying the water with the carbon dioxide, which is important for the next step.

3. This solution will also turn a blue compound yellow almost instantly. Hold up the bottle of bromothymol blue so you can see the color. Add a dash of bromothymol blue to your bubbling Toobe. The indicator will turn yellow almost immediately.

4. Once the solution has turned a light yellow, pour the liquid contents into the second Toobe and leave the dry ice in the first Toobe. The blue solution that turned yellow is actually neither color. It is green. Take the pipette and fill it with sodium hydroxide. Carefully add a drop at a time. You will notice that, as you near a pH of 7, the color starts to become sea-green. Add one or two more drops and stir the contents of the Toobe. If you hit the pH perfectly, you will have a Toobe full of green liquid.

If you add too much base (sodium hydroxide or whatever you are using) you will zip right past the green color and the solution will turn blue. That might be entertaining, but it doesn't follow the story line. Go slowly and stir after each drop to get the full plot.

5. Finally, pour the green liquid back into the Toobe with the dry ice and stopper it. As the gas pressure inside the Toobe builds, it will push on the stopper. When it gets high enough, it will shoot the stopper into the air. *Voila ...* You have a color-changing cannon and all the associated pandemonium to go with it.

When it comes time to insert the stopper, add only enough water to fill the Toobe two-thirds full. You want to have some room for the gas to accumulate and build up pressure. If it is too full, the stopper will shoot out, but it will not be as dramatic.

How Come, Huh?

Bromothymol blue, also known as dibromothymolsulfon-phthalein, is an acid base indicator that operates in a pH range of 6.0 to 7.6. When it is in a basic solution, it exhibits a blue color. When neutral, it is green. When slightly acidic, it is yellow. As the piece of dry ice releases the gases, the carbon dioxide acidifies the water. The more carbon dioxide that bubbles through the water, the lower the pH gets. When it reaches a neutral level, it turns green, and when it becomes acidic, it turns yellow. When the sodium hydroxide is added, a couple of drops at a time, this base causes the pH to rise again. The color changes back to blue and starts over again.

Science Fair Extensions

17. There are 25 or 30 different chemical indicators. Grab a Merck index and try other indicators for other color sequences.

Patriotic Electron Clouds

The Experiment

Ah, the old red, white, and blue—the foundation for designing Old Glory and a reminder of our great heritage and the sacrifices that our ancestors made. If you live in Tonga and are reading this without much of a clue, we understand.

We have been experimenting with our toy chemistry set and have accidentally stumbled upon a reaction that is truly American in color. When we run an electric current through a special slurry that we have concocted, the solution divides itself into red, white, and blue sections according to the polar orientation of the specific ions. So, just what is responsible for this burst of patriotism? Let's find out.

Materials

1   1 oz. bottle of dehydrated gel
1   1 oz. bottle of potassium ferrocyanide
1   1 oz. bottle of phenolphthalein in alcohol
1   Clear, plastic blister (small tub)
        or cereal bowl
2   #8 ungalvanized nails
2   Alligator clips
1   D cell battery
1   D cell battery clip
1   Craft stick
     Water

Procedure

1. Open the bottle of dehydrated gel and add about half a capful to the plastic blister or cereal bowl. Then add a capful of phenolphthalein and a capful of potassium ferrocyanide to the gel.

2. Fill the blister/bowl with water until it is about a quarter of an inch deep. Stir the whole concoction. You will notice that as you stir, the gel begins to absorb the liquid and produce a slushy mix that looks like a tub full of runny grits. Don't panic; this is good, even for a Northerner. If the gel starts to set up and get firm, add small amounts of water until you return to the runny-grits consistency so coveted in this lab activity.

3. Snap the battery into its holder and connect an alligator clip to each battery terminal. The alligator clips are so named because they tend to resemble the shape of an alligator head—at least if you're in low light and if it has been a very long day. Pinch the back end of the clip to open the jaws, and clamp a small nail inside the teeth of each clip.

4. Place the nails in the gel mixture, about an inch from each other. Be sure they don't touch. Observe what happens near each of the nails.

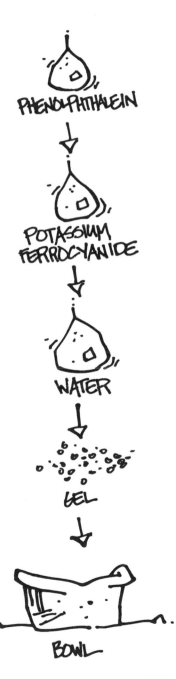

PHENOLPHTHALEIN

POTASSIUM FERROCYANIDE

WATER

GEL

BOWL

Patriotic Electron Clouds

Data & Observations

Draw a picture of what you see in the blister / bowl in the space provided below.

How Come, Huh?

The battery produces a current that flows into the positively charged nail through the gel mixture and back into the negatively charged nail. When an electric current flows through water, it breaks down, forming positive and negative ions. The negative ions are attracted to the positive nail and the positive ions head for the negative nail. That's just the way it works.

Phenolphthalein is an acid base indicator. When it comes in contact with the positive hydroxide ions, the pH in that area increases, and the color of the indicator changes to pink. The opposite is true at the other pole where the negative ions congregate, react with the potassium ferrocyanide, and result in a blue color.

The Chemistry Behind It

The water is reduced at the negative terminal, or cathode, by electrons from the nail to form hydrogen gas and basic hydroxide ions:

$$4H_2O \text{ (l)} + 4e^- \rightarrow 2H_2 \text{ (g)} + 4OH^- \text{ (aq)}$$

The basic hydroxide ions that form at the cathode react with the phenolphthalein indicator, changing the gel from colorless to pink around the nail:

$$
\begin{array}{ccccc}
C_{20}H_{14}O_4 & + & 2NaOH & \rightarrow & Na_2C_{20}H_{12}O_4 \\
\textit{Phenolphthalein} & + & \textit{Sodium Hydroxide} & \rightarrow & \textit{Sodium Salt} \\
& & & & \textit{(pink)}
\end{array}
$$

The iron in the nail is oxidized at the positive terminal, or anode, to form iron ions:

$$Fe \text{ (s)} \rightarrow Fe^{2+} \text{ (aq)} + 2e^-$$

The iron ions then react with the potassium ferrocyanide to form the blue complex known as Turnbull's Blue:

$$Fe^{2+} \text{ (aq)} + K_4[Fe(CN)_6] \text{ (aq)} \rightarrow KFe[Fe(CN)_6] \bullet H_2O$$

Disappearing Ink

The Experiment

This is a magician's stand-by. An acid base indicator by the name of thymolpthalein is changed from clear to blue using a strong base—in this case, sodium hydroxide. The "ink" is then squirted onto a white shirt, blouse, or other article of clothing. The magician reassures the offended party that the ink will soon disappear and, sure enough, in a matter of seconds, the blue stain dissolves into the fabric and order is once again restored to the universe.

Materials

1   1 oz. bottle of thymolphthalein in ethanol
1   1 oz. bottle of sodium hydroxide solution (1M)
1   Small paint brush
1   Sheet of white paper
1   Pair of rubber gloves
1   Plastic pipette
1   Set of lungs with lots of carbon dioxide
1   Old white sock, preferably clean
1   Pair of goggles (optional)

Procedure

1. Gloves on! Slap those babies on your fingers and cover your eyes if you have goggles.

2. Take the caps off the bottles. Fill the pipette with liquid from the sodium hydroxide bottle and slowly add drops of the clear liquid, one at a time, to the bottle of thymolphthalein. After each drop, gently swirl the bottle of thymolpthalein to mix the two chemicals.

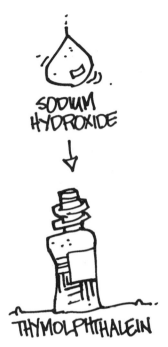

You will notice that when you add each drop, the clear solution will turn dark blue for a second or two and then return to the clear color. When the solution turns dark blue and stays that way after you have swirled it several times, stop adding the sodium hydroxide. **Your solution is perfectly balanced. If you add too much sodium hydroxide, it will take a lot longer for the ink to disappear.**

3. Rinse your pipette thoroughly with water and dip it into the fresh batch of disappearing ink you've just made. Squirt the ink onto some white fabric.—Socks work well. Observe the ink.

4. Repeat the experiment in a different place. Blow on the ink and see if this speeds the disappearing act or slows it down. If you are confident in your running skills and the track coach at your school salivates at the thought of you anchoring the 4 x 100 relay, squirt some ink on a white shirt or blouse as it passes by.

5. Take the paint brush and write a secret message on a sheet of white paper. Let it dry. To make the message reappear, moisten the paper with a little bit of ammonia or sodium hydroxide. Any strong, basic liquid will cause the ink to reappear.

Disappearing Ink

6. If you want to have some fun, write a message on a large sheet of white paper and let it dry—something like, "Happy Birthday, Mom!" When your mom walks into the room, use a spray bottle full of ammonia to squirt onto the white paper. Your message will appear as if by magic.

How Come, Huh?

Thymolphthalein (pronounced *thigh • mole • thay • lean*) is an acid base indicator. When the solution is basic, it is a deep blue color, but when it becomes neutral or slightly acidic, it disappears, becoming clear.

Carbon dioxide is present in the air we breathe in fairly large quantities. Carbon dioxide is also slightly acidic. It lowers the pH of the solutions that it comes in contact with in a short amount of time. Because the blue color is created using sodium hydroxide and because it decomposes to sodium carbonate during the reaction, you have nothing to worry about if it gets on your clothes. Sodium carbonate is just washing soda. Another wonder of science.

The Chemistry Behind It

Another chemical equation that describes another mystery...

chemical in bottle 1 / is added to / chemical in bottle 2 / making / dark blue liquid / and / water, or:

$$C_{28}H_{30}O_4 \text{(liquid)} + NaOH \text{(aq)} \rightarrow Na_2C_{28}H_{28}O_4 \text{(aq)} + 2H_2O$$

thymolphthalein + sodium hydroxide → thymolphthalein + water

then ... *drum roll please,*

dark blue liquid / comes in contact with / invisible gas / making / washing soda / and / clear liquid:

$$Na_2C_{28}H_{28}O_4 \text{(aq)} + CO_2 \text{(aq)} \rightarrow Na_2CO_3 \text{(aq)} + C_{28}H_{30}O_4$$

thymolphthalein + carbon dioxide → sodium carbonate + thymolphthalein

Another mystery solved, the union is intact, and character is restored.

Bloody Fingerprints

The Experiment

Your lab partner, Miss Cristal Balle, noted paranormal explorer and part-time Internet psychic hostess, claims to have recovered blood from a ghost. According to Miss Balle, ghost blood is clear until it comes in contact with human flesh. When that happens, the spirit of the ghost invades the body of the innocent participant and "borrows" a few corpuscles of living red blood to make its presence known.

To prove her claim, she poured a small sample of the ghost blood on a plain, white napkin, rolled her fingers in the clear liquid, and then applied her fingertip to a sheet of golden paper. Blood instantly appeared! Or did it? You're the detective… Time for a little lab work.

Materials

1   1 oz. bottle of sodium hydroxide, dilute
1   Sheet of goldenrod paper
1   Paper towel
1   Magnifying lens

FINGER

SODIUM HYDROXIDE

GOLDENROD PAPER

Procedure

1. Pour two capfuls of ghost blood, which has been mislabeled as "sodium hydroxide," onto the towel. Use just enough to get the paper towel damp.

2. Roll your index finger in the ghost blood so that it is moist but not dripping wet. Then roll the same finger across the surface of the goldenrod paper. You should see a blood-red fingerprint when you lift your finger off the paper.

3. Make a full set of prints, labeling each print with the name of the finger that made it. Don't forget your thumbs. Compare your prints with the list found on the FBI website showing the different characteristics of fingerprints.

How Come, Huh?

Here are the clues that will help you start to unravel what really happened. Sodium hydroxide is a strong base, a chemical compound with a pH of about 10. Goldenrod paper is manufactured using phenolphthalein. When phenolphthalein is exposed to a chemical with a pH above 8, it turns blood-red.

So, in putting all these clues together, it works like this: When the golden paper was made, a chemical was added to it. This chemical appears colorless unless it comes in contact with a strong base. You rolled your finger in a strong base, sodium hydroxide, and then transferred that base directly to the paper. When the base came in contact with the chemical, it turned blood-red. No corpuscles were snached from your body. Instead, it was a chemical reaction between the sodium hydroxide (ghost blood) and the phenolphthalein in the paper.

The Chemistry Behind It

So you are asking yourself if there is a chemical equation that describes this mystery and, of course, there is. Here you go, first in words and then in chemical shorthand for beginners:

Chemical in paper / is touched by / clear liquid on finger / making / pink spots / and / water, or:

$$C_{28}H_{30}O_4 \text{(liquid)} + NaOH \text{(aq)} \rightarrow Na_2C_{28}H_{28}O_4 \text{(aq)} + 2H_2O$$
phenolphthalein + sodium hydroxide → phenolphthalein + water

Rainbow Bouquet

The Experiment

Your neighbor likes white silk flowers. They match everything in his house. However, when he cleans near the flowers with bleach or ammonia, they instantly turn pink. This tends to unnerve the poor old boy. He has found that if he immediately places the flowers in vinegar, they return to their white color. That is, until he cleans again. Drives the poor guy nuts. Figure out what is going on and help your neighbor solve his mystery.

Materials

1   White silk flower
1   1 oz. bottle of sodium hydroxide solution (1M)
1   1 oz. bottle of acetic acid
1   Small paint brush
1   Pair of rubber gloves
     Water

Procedure

1. Dip the paint brush into the solution of sodium hydroxide and touch it to the petals of the silk flower. Observe what happens when the liquid comes in contact with the fabric.

2. Rinse the paint brush in water and then dip it in vinegar. Paint the vinegar onto the same portion of the flower that you painted the sodium hydroxide onto and see if there is any effect on the pink that was produced.

3. Experiment with painting your flower with strong bases that are used for cleaning and acids that are used for cooking. When you are all done with the flower, you can save it. It can be used over and over.

Data & Observations

Make a list of cleaning compounds you find around your house and test them on the white, silk flower. Be sure that you have your parents' permission before you test anything. In the *Reaction* column, record whether the flower turned pink or remained white.

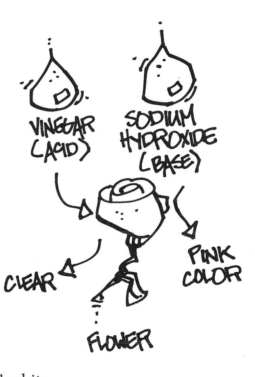

Liquid Tested	Reaction
1. Sodium Hydroxide	
2. Ammonia	
3. Acetic Acid (Vinegar)	
4.	
5.	
6.	

Rainbow Bouquet

How Come, Huh?

It turns out that the silk flower has been dipped into a chemical called phenolphthalein. Phenolphthalein is primarily used as an acid base indicator and changes color from clear to pink and back again. And if you happen to be a veterinarian, it also makes a great laxative, but that's another lab.

If phenolphthalein is in an acidic solution like vinegar, it appears colorless. If it is in a basic solution like ammonia, bleach, or even sodium hydroxide, it appears pink in color. Once the flower has turned pink, you can render it colorless by adding acid to the pink area and lowering the pH again.

The Chemistry Behind It

$$C_{20}H_{14}O_4\,(S) \quad + \quad 2NaOH\,(aq) \leftrightarrow Na_2C_{20}H_{12}O_4\,(aq) + 2H_2O$$
phenolphthalein + sodium hydroxide ↔ sodium + salt
(colorless) *(pink)*

$$Na_2C_{20}H_{12}O_4\,(aq) + H_2SO_4\,(aq) \leftrightarrow C_{20}H_{14}O_4\,(aq) + Na_2SO_4\,(aq)$$
sodium salt + sulfuric acid ↔ phenolphthalein + sodium sulfate
(pink) *(colorless)*

How to Prepare the Silk Flower

Finding a silk flower is easy. You can purchase it at virtually any craft or hobby store. They sell them for faux flower arrangements; the cost should be around $1.95 for a dozen.

Start with a quart of ethanol, available at the hardware store, and add 0.4g of phenolphthalein powder to the alcohol. Shake the container for 30 seconds to dissolve the powder.

Go outside where it is well ventilated, pour the mix into a shallow pan, and dip the flower. Set it on a hard surface to dry. It will be ready to go in 15 minutes.

Pink Kisses Never Lie

The Experiment

This is a wonderful lab activity for learning more about pH, acid base indicators, and the hazards of communicable diseases. You'll work in a group. Each kid in your group is going to be given a pipette and a test tube full of a clear liquid. Once everything is passed out, tell your friends that they get to "kiss" two other people in the group. (For the record, you need at least ten folks to make this work well.) After everyone kisses, you'll discover that one of the kids has a "cold." Your job is to figure out how many kids are "infected."

Materials

1   1 oz. bottle of sodium hydroxide
1   1 oz. bottle of phenolphthalein
10   Test tubes
10   Pipettes
     Water

SODIUM HYDROXIDE

LIQUID WITH PHENOLPHTHALEIN

PINK COLOR

Procedure

1. Before anyone joins your group, fill one of the test tubes half full with sodium hydroxide. Fill the remainder of the test tubes with an equal amount of water.

2. When you are ready to begin, hand each of your friends a test tube and a pipette. Tell them that they are to "kiss" two other people in the group. Everyone has to kiss two people—no more, no fewer.

The way that you kiss someone is to take a big snootful of liquid from your container and squirt it into the other person's test tube; that person will give you a snootful back.

Pink Kisses Never Lie

3. After everyone has finished kissing two people, tell them that someone in the group has a cold. To find out who has been exposed to the cold, they will all have to undergo a test.

4. Have group members hold their test tubes in front of them. Open the bottle of phenolphthalein and squeeze until your dropper is full. Using the pipette, test the tubes, one at a time. Test them by adding two or three drops of the phenolphthalein to each tube. If it turns bright pink, the friend with that tube has been infected. If it remains clear, that friend is off the hook.

Data & Observations

Number of people in the group: _____

Number that tested positive: _____

Percentage that may get sick: _____%

How Come, Huh?

Phenolphthalein turns bright pink in the presence of a strong base. The person that had the sodium hydroxide (the strong base) was the one who was infected. Anyone who "kissed" the infected person runs the risk of getting the cold. Not only that, but anyone who kissed someone who kissed the infected person also runs the risk of getting the cold.

Big Idea 7

Short, stumpity groups of molecules (called mers) can combine to form very long chains of molecules (called polymers). These molecules are characterized by their gooey, sticky ability to stretch and form long, elastic compounds that ooze and drip all over the place.

Collapsible Coffee Cups

The Experiment

A styrofoam cup is going to be placed in an aluminum tart pan. A small quantity of clear liquid is poured into the cup, and the cup disappears … almost. Amazing and true.

Materials

1   5 inch tart pan
1   6 oz. polystyrene coffee cup
1   Set of fingers
1   Bottle of acetone

Procedure

1.   Gently place the cup upright in the center of the tart pan.

2.   Pour about half an ounce of acetone into the cup and observe what happens. Look for bubbles of gas and the sound of fizzing near the base of the coffee cup.

3.   When the cup appears to be completely "dissolved" (our apologies to the chemists of the world), pull the blob out and play with it. The acetone won't hurt your hands but it may dry out your skin a little bit. In fact, if you look at your skin after you have touched the acetone, you will notice a faint, whitish residue. That's fat from the subcutaneous layer of your skin. Don't get smart and think that you can lose a lot of weight by sitting in a tub of acetone. It only affects the fat that it can get to easily, just under your skin.

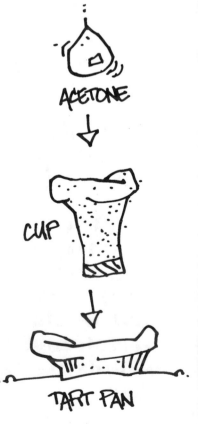

ACETONE

CUP

TART PAN

4. When you are done, you can either toss the plastic into the recycling bin or let it dry, color it, and give it to your mom as a present.

How Come, Huh?

As soon as the acetone hits the cup, it begins to coagulate, or dissolve, the polystyrene. The acetone is chemically squishing the air out of the spaces in the plastic and, in no time, the cup becomes a blob of styrene.

First of all, let's pick apart this "styrofoam" word. "Styro" is short for a type of plastic called styrene, which is used extensively in the manufacture of plastics because it is easy to combine with other molecules. The word "foam" suggests that we have another col-loid—a "plastic foam" that was created when a gas (air) was dispersed into a solid (polystyrene).

If we look at the process of creating styrofoam, we find this is true. As the polystyrene was being molded to form the cup, gas was injected into the mixture of plastic and was then trapped in the spaces as it cooled. This trapped air is what allows polystyrene to insulate so well. The acetone causes the polystyrene molecules to unhook from one another, and they just collapse.

Science Fair Extensions

18. This reaction is the same for all kinds of styrofoam. Take a gallon jar and fill it with a quart of acetone (available from the local hardware store for a couple of bucks) and start adding styrofoam peanuts. You will be able to add several thousand before the container gets even slightly full.

Thyxophyllic Goo

The Experiment

A small amount of water is going to be added to a pile of dry cornstarch that is in the palm of your hand. As you gently work the water into the cornstarch, it starts to form a ball. As long as you keep pressure on the ball of cornstarch, it looks and behaves like a solid. As soon as you take the pressure off and stop rolling the ball around in your hand, it turns into a runny, gooey mess that oozes all over your hand.

Materials

1   Box of cornstarch
2   Hands

      Water in a cup

Procedure

1.   Pour a small pile of cornstarch into your hand. For the more precise, a small pile would be a heaping teaspoon.

2.   You want to add water to the corn-starch very slowly—add too much and you won't get the desired effect. Start by dipping your fingers into the water and then dribbling it onto the pile of cornstarch. As you dribble, "pinch" the water into the cornstarch, forming a ball.

3.   When you get to the point where you can roll the ball of cornstarch between your two palms, you have added enough water.

4.   Pick the ball up in your fingers and hold it over your open hand. You will notice that the solid ball of cornstarch turns to a liquid and drips down into your hand.

5. When you are done, toss the whole mess into the sink and rinse it down the drain with hot water or toss it into the garbage can.

How Come, Huh?

When you keep pressure on the ball of cornstarch, it acts like a solid. When you ease up and reduce the pressure, it acts like a liquid. You can bet that there is a name for this kind of compound.

The word "thyxophyllic" means "pressure loving," definitely a Type A compound. Cornstarch is composed of very long molecules. (Think of them as strands of spaghetti.) When the water is added to the cornstarch, a colloid is formed because the strands float around in the water but do not react with it. The interesting thing about cornstarch molecules is that if you squish them, they get all tangled up and can't move. This is why the ball feels like a solid when you roll it around in the palm of your hand. As soon as you take the pressure off, the molecules of cornstarch are free to move around in and among the water molecules again. This is why they flow easily from place to place and behave like a liquid.

Science Fair Extensions

19. Make a mixture of cornstarch and water inside a 3 to 5 gallon tub. Take your hand and plunge it into the cornstarch without any problems. Now take a hammer and hit the surface. Different reaction, no?

Pseudo Silly Putty

The Experiment

Ordinary white glue is going to be added to Borax to make an extraordinary batch of glue glop that you can bounce, press onto paper, and hang from your ear.

Materials

1   1 oz. bottle of glue solution (50%)
1   1 oz. bottle of 2% sodium tetraborate
1   5 oz. wax cup
1   Plastic, sealable baggie
1   Craft stick
1   Bottle of food coloring

Procedure

1.   Shake the glue solution for 20 seconds before you open the bottle, because this stuff settles when it sits around. Pour half of the glue from the bottle into the wax cup.

2.   Add 1 capful of sodium tetraborate to the glue solution and, using the craft stick, stir with reckless abandon until a blob starts to form. This usually takes 15 to 20 seconds.

3.   When most of the liquid has turned into a rubbery blob that is clinging to the craft stick, pull the whole mess out of the cup and peel it off with your fingers. Roll the glue glop around in the palm of your hand.

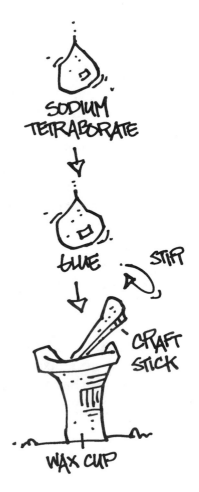

SODIUM TETRABORATE

GLUE   STIR

CRAFT STICK

WAX CUP

4. Time to experiment. Try bouncing the blob on the table. Find an old newspaper and make an impression of the text or pictures by pressing the blob onto the paper. Let it hang and stretch from your nose, ear, or other body appendage. Have fun.

5. When you are done, put it in a sealable plastic bag so it won't dry out and save it for a rainy day. If you are not a hoarder, you can toss the glop into the garbage without fear of contaminating the world's water supply.

How Come, Huh?

Glue molecules are long, rubbery, sticky molecules. Think of them as strands of spaghetti or, if you prefer, snakes. The sodium tetraborate cross-links the glue molecules, which means that it acts a lot like the rungs of a ladder. Without the rungs, the ladder would just be two long sticks. With the rungs, the ladder becomes connected. The Borax connects the long glue molecules into a large, 3-dimensional net that remains free to move about.

The "net's" ability to bounce is just a function of the elasticity of the molecules. They hit the floor and absorb the energy. The ball of molecules rebounds, or gives the energy back, and bounces off the floor or table.

Slime

The Experiment

A green, slippery liquid is mixed with a blue liquid. As the two are stirred together, they form a slippery, slimy, green colloid that is known by various names: slime, pseudo snot, goo. Not to be outdone, we call it frog phlegm. You choose.

Materials

1   2 oz. bottle of 2% polyvinyl alcohol solution
1   1 oz. bottle of 2% sodium tetraborate solution
1   5 oz. wax cup
1   Craft stick

Procedure

1.   Pour half of the polyvinyl alcohol into the wax cup. Be sure to save the other half of the solution for an experiment that you'll do later in the book.

2.   Add one capful of sodium tetraborate. Stir like crazy and you should notice that the more you stir, the slimier your solution becomes. If you have stirred for 30 seconds and your mixture is still a little runny, add a couple more drops of sodium tetraborate. If you add too much of the sodium tetraborate, your frog phlegm will become brittle and a little crumbly, and we want fresh, vibrant phlegm, not the stuff that's been on the bottom of the chair for a day.

SODIUM TETRABORATE

POLYVINYL ALCOHOL

STIR

CRAFT STICK

WAX CUP

3. Once you get your phlegm to the desired consistency, play with it. Let it drip, hold it up to your nose and fake a sneeze, rip it in half and then put it back together again.

4. When you're all done, save your phlegm by putting it in a sealable baggie for another rainy day. For longer life, toss the baggie in the fridge to retard bacterial growth. Or, huck it in the garbage can. It is 98% water and will dry to a thin, green layer of stuff.

How Come, Huh?

Polyvinyl alcohol is the primary ingredient in contact lens wetting solution, and sodium tetraborate is common household Borax, a whitener that is added to laundry—neither of which should pose a health risk to anyone. Occasionally, someone will ask us what would happen if a kid ate this stuff. Being mostly water and hydrocarbons, our best guess is that nothing would happen. Our next best guess is that the kid would have a big, green, slippery poop in a day or so. Either way, the band would play on.

Polyvinyl alcohol is made up of long, long molecules that are floating in water—bowl of spaghetti or pool full of snakes. The tetraborate solution hooks the long chains of molecules together, and a big, flexible, 3-dimensional net is formed. Artificial snot that is bacteria-free is yours for the mixing. Could life really get any better?

Monster Snot

The Experiment

Guar gum, which is used as an additive to thicken foods like ice cream, is going to be combined with ordinary Borax, known in scientific circles as sodium tetraborate. When this happens, a light green, rubbery but not-too-slimy blob of jiggling monster snot will form. We can't verify that this is exactly what monster snot would be like because we haven't actually ever dug around in the nose of a real live monster to compare it, but this is close enough to the real thing for us. If you are brave enough to do the field research to see if we're right, drop us a line with your observations.

Materials

1   1 oz. bottle of guar gum powder
1   1 oz. bottle of sodium tetraborate
1   Craft stick
1   5 oz. wax cup
    Water

Procedure

1. Take the cap off the bottle of guar gum. You will notice that this is a fine, white powder. Fill the cap half-full with this powder and empty it into the wax cup.

2. To the powder, add three ounces of water, just a little more than half the cup, and stir the water and powder together with the craft stick.

3. Add two capfuls of the liquid sodium tetraborate and keep stirring. The monster snot will start to form immediately.

4. When the snot gets to a nice rubbery consistency, empty it out into your hand and play with it.

5. When you are all done, you can toss it in the garbage.

How Come, Huh?

When the water, guar gum, and Borax are all mixed together, they form a rubbery, jiggly blob of light-blue colored colloid. A colloid, which you have been making and playing with for the last four experiments, is a mixture of two compounds. The mixture can be a gas into a gas, a solid into a gas (hairspray and deodorant), a liquid into a liquid (Sterno and hair gel), gases into solids (styrofoams), or any other combination of solids, liquids, and gases that you can think of. The main thing is that colloids are mixtures, not compounds.

In this experiment, the sodium tetraborate actually hooks the long guar gum molecules together, not unlike the way it operated in the pseudo silly putty and slime experiments. This hooking together of molecules is characteristic of both colloids and polymers. Long chains of molecules are hooked together in a variety of ways to make amorphous blobs of glop. Now that's chemistry at its finest.

Colloidal Mushrooms

The Experiment

Kids always seem to want to take all the leftover chemicals and mix them in a big pile to see what happens. Invariably this idea is vetoed by the teacher, but today, as the grand finale for this set of lab ideas, we are going to do just that. Four of the chemicals that you have used to make that cool foam and that gooey frog phlegm are going to be mixed into a common container, which will produce… well, you'll see.

Materials

1   2 oz. bottle of 2% polyvinyl alcohol solution
1   1 oz. bottle of 2% sodium tetraborate solution
1   1 oz. bottle of aluminum sulfate powder
1   1 oz. bottle of sodium bicarbonate powder
2   5 oz. wax cups
1   Tart pan
1   Craft stick

Procedure

1. Pour the remaining ounce of polyvinyl alcohol into a wax cup and add two caps of baking soda. Stir the soda into the solution with the craft stick until all of the lumps are gone. Add a half ounce of water and stir some more. Set the cup in the center of the tart pan.

2. Pour half a bottle of sodium tetraborate into the second wax cup and add one cap of aluminum sulfate powder. Stir the powder into the solution with the craft stick to remove the lumps here also. Add a half ounce of water and stir some more.

3. Pour the contents of the second cup into the first and observe what happens as all four of the chemicals mix and react with one another.

How Come, Huh?

This experiment is a combination of two of the previous experiments. Polyvinyl alcohol and sodium tetraborate combine to form a gooey, slimy polymer. This polymer is flexible and acts like a big net, trapping the gas that was produced by the reaction that is described next.

The aluminum sulfate combines with the sodium bicarbonate to produce and release lots of carbon dioxide gas. (Please refer to the orange sorbet reaction.) This gas expands and gets trapped in the frog phlegm (slime) making one big, colloidal mushroom that oozes up and out of the cup and over into the tart pan.

The whole mess can be tossed into the garbage or washed down the sink after you have had fun with your colloidal mushroom.

Science Fair Extensions

20. Head to the store and find a kit called "Make Your Own Bouncy Balls." This is a great polymer kit.

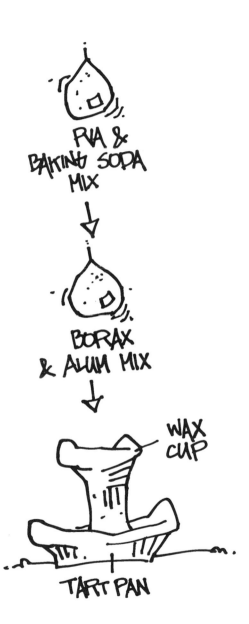

PVA & BAKING SODA MIX

BORAX & ALUM MIX

WAX CUP

TART PAN

Big Idea 8

Some chemicals react with air and oxidize rapidly to produce large amounts of heat, light, and quite often, sound.

Smokescreen on Demand

The Experiment

This experiment actually falls into the life skills category, especially if you aspire to be just like James Bond. After all, every good agent needs to know how to make a smokescreen so he or she can get away.

You are going to mix ammonium nitrate, zinc dust, and water to create the smokescreen. When the three are combined, they produce what is called an exothermic reaction—one that produces lots of heat. You will also produce nitrogen gas, zinc oxide, and water vapor that will form the smokescreen.

Materials

1   0.5 oz. bottle of zinc dust (dark powder)
1   0.5 oz. bottle of ammonium nitrate (white powder)
1   Plastic pipette
1   Bottle cap without the plastic liner
1   Small pie tin, 5 inch diameter
1   5 oz. wax cup
1   Pair of rubber gloves
    Water

Procedure

1. Put your goggles on. Fill the glass with water, then **go outside and find an open area to work in.** Place the bottle cap in that open area, away from buildings.

Smokescreen on Demand

2. Open the bottle of ammonium nitrate. Pour two capfuls of ammonium nitrate into the bottle cap. Then recap the bottle.

3. Now open the bottle of zinc dust and sprinkle half a capful of zinc on top of the ammonium nitrate. Then recap the bottle of zinc.

WATER

ZINC DUST

AMMONIUM NITRATE

TART PAN

Using the craft stick, gently mix the two chemicals together.

4. Add two drops of water to the pile of chemicals in the bottle cap and immediately move five to six feet away. It takes a little while for the reaction to get going (sometimes more than a minute) so be patient.

One caution that we do have is that if you add too much water, you will produce a bubbling, grey mudpot that might burp a little steam but will not produce the large volumes of smoke that you desire. Add two drops and then hang in there while everything reacts.

5. Once the reaction has been completed and your smokescreen is another fond "oooh, aaah" memory, use caution as you pick up the materials. The bottle cap gets very hot during the reaction and has a tendency to scorch fingers.

How Come, Huh?

The water allows the two chemicals to go into solution. When this happens, the ions are free to react with one another and, in this case, the ammonium nitrate and zinc dust react to liberate nitrogen gas, water vapor, and zinc oxide. Zinc oxide, for the record, is that white stuff that you see some folks smearing on their noses to prevent burning.

The exothermic part of this reaction is the fact that heat is produced when the chemical bonds are broken. The fact that heat is produced, a gas is released, and the color of the leftover components has changed, indicates that a chemical reaction has just taken place right before your eyes. And some people think James Bond is just a sexy counterintelligence spy.

The Chemistry Behind It

NH_4NO_3 (s) + Zn (s) – N_2 (g) + ZnO (s) + $2H_2O$ (g) + Heat

ammonium nitrate + zinc - nitrogen + zinc oxide + water

Water Cannon

The Experiment

Calcium carbide, itself, is not terribly interesting. It's a white, lumpy chemical that just sits there. However, stick it in a closed container, douse it with water, introduce a flame, and you have a whole different can of tomatoes.

You are going to make a cannon that runs on water, or at least reacts with it. Soup cans are hollowed out and taped together. A Nerf ball is stuffed in one end, and water is added to the other. The only thing that you're missing is a match flame, then *voila*, flying Nerf ball, barking dogs, and cats scampering for the nearest tree.

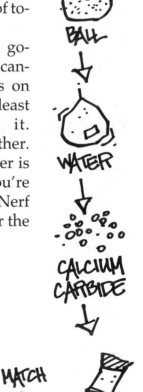

Materials

4 Soup cans, # 303, empty
1 Can opener
1 Roll of duct tape
1 Bottle of calcium chloride
1 Book of matches
1 Hammer
1 Nail, 16 penny
1 Nerf ball, round
Water

Procedure

1. Remove both ends from three of the four soup cans and just the top from the fourth can. Clean all the cans out with soap and water. Be careful. The cut metal may be sharp.

2. Place the can that still has the base on the table. Center a second can on top of it and tape it in place with the duct tape.

3. Place the third and fourth cans on top of the first two and tape them in place so that you have a long, metal tube.

4. Using the nail and hammer, punch a hole two-thirds of the way up the bottom can.

5. Add a capful of calcium chloride to the bottom of the metal tube. Add 3 or 4 ounces of water to the calcium chloride and seal the tube with the Nerf ball.

6. Wait about 20 seconds for the hydrogen gas to accumulate. Then, holding the tube at a 45° angle and away from all onlookers, insert the match flame into the hole. If all goes well, you will hear a loud "boom" and the Nerf ball will be accelerating away from you.

How Come, Huh?

The calcium chloride reacts with the water to liberate hydrogen gas. Hydrogen gas is flammable, so when you introduce the match to the chamber, the gas ignites. When gas heats, the pressure inside the container increases. The ball can no longer hold the expanding gas back, so it shoves the ball out into the room and the expanding air escapes rapidly, producing compressed sound waves, which account for the "boom." New Year's Eve will never be the same again.

Baster Blaster

The Experiment

You can demonstrate how thunder is created and make Thanksgiving a whole lot more fun in your house at the same time. This experiment allows you to create a controlled reaction in a rubber bulb that will launch a Ping-Pong ball into the air with a loud bang. The lab demonstrates how superheated air expands rapidly, causing a bang. Thunder is produced in the same way.

Materials

1   Turkey baster
1   Kitchen knife
1   Lantern ignitor
1   Ping-Pong ball
1   Eyedropper
1   Bottle of isopropyl alcohol
    Adult Supervision

Procedure

1.   Remove the rubber bulb from a turkey baster. Using a sharp kitchen knife, carefully cut a small "X" in the side of the bulb. Use the illustration at the right to help you locate the correct spot.

2.   A lantern ignitor can be purchased from a sporting goods store. Remove the nut from the end and thread the shaft through the "X" that you made in the side of the bulb. Replace the nut. Use the illustration at the bottom right as a guide.

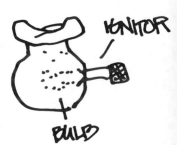

3.   Squeeze the center of an eyedropper that is full of isopropyl alcohol inside the bulb. Swirl the alcohol around a bit.

4. Place the Ping-Pong ball inside the opening of the baster.

5. Pointing the ball away from yourself and others, give the ignitor a quick twist and the ball will shoot into the air with a loud, high "pop."

How Come, Huh?

Isopropyl alcohol is a flammable liquid. When you squirted the liquid into the rubber bulb, it started to vaporize almost instantly, making it even more flammable.

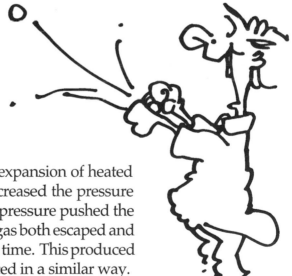

Placing the Ping-Pong ball in the mouth of the baster created a closed system, trapping the flammable gas inside the bulb. When you flipped the ignitor switch, a spark was generated. The spark ignited the alcohol vapor, which expanded rapidly. This rapid expansion of heated gas inside the baster bulb increased the pressure dramatically. The increased pressure pushed the ball out and the compressed gas both escaped and expanded rapidly at the same time. This produced a "bang." Thunder is produced in a similar way.

Science Fair Extensions

21. Take the idea and adapt it to different-sized containers with different balls. Nerf balls work great because you can cram them into small spaces. Use your imagination and work carefully.

Lycopodium Flash

The Experiment

Lycopodium powder is a favorite of Hollywood's special effects people. It is an extremely flammable powder that is easy to ignite. It creates a huge ball of fire but relatively little heat and no poisonous by-products. Not bad for a spore from a lowly club moss ... such humble beginnings.

We are going to show you how to create a controlled fireball that will impress your friends and relatives and provide more "ooh, aahs" than most of the fireworks that you can purchase for the nation's birthday.

Materials

1	Pair of goggles
1	Propane torch
1	Ignitor
1	Bottle of lycopodium powder
1	Fire blanket and/or fire extinguisher
	Adult Supervision

Procedure

1.   Goggles on, gloves on. Make sure that you are in an area that is free of flammable materials. Be sure to follow all safety procedures and, if a fire extinguisher or fire blanket is handy, have it available.

2.   You will also want to do this in a well ventilated area. Some folks who tend to have allergies to things like pollen and grass may react to the spores in the air. It is uncommon, but you might as well be prepared.

3. Place the torch on a flat table that has had everything removed from its surface. Ignite the torch. Be sure to have an adult present.

4. Pour a small pile of lycopodium powder, about a table-spoonful, into the palm of your hand. Close your hand and, standing three to four feet from the flame, toss the powder directly at the flame but not toward anyone who is observing the experiment.

If everything goes according to plan, the lycopodium will disperse into the flame, ignite, and create a large flash of light and fire before it dissipates. It should look something like the cartoon pictured above.

How Come, Huh?

The lycopodium powder is a fine powder. When you throw it into the air, it gets mixed with oxygen and is introduced to a flame that is well above its kindling point. Heat, oxygen, and fuel dispersed over a very large surface area make for a great reaction.

Cornstarch Fireballs

The Experiment

This was the very first science demo that I used in the classroom, and it remains my all-time favorite for several reasons: One, it produces a huge, relatively harmless ball of fire, which everyone loves to see. Two, kids absolutely love it. And, three, it is an excellent way to learn about lab safety.

Materials

1   Propane torch w/ignitor
2   Pairs of goggles
1   Pair of gloves, heavy
1   Box of cornstarch
1   Fire blanket and/or fire extinguisher
1   Sheet of paper
Adult Supervision

Procedure

1.   Goggles on. Have an adult light the propane torch. The flame needs to be as big as possible.

2.   Set a sheet of photocopy paper on the table and pour a pile of cornstarch in the middle of it. A handful will do. With the help of an adult, attempt to light the cornstarch on fire with the torch. It will brown but it will not catch on fire because there is not enough oxygen present for the cornstarch to reach the kindling point.

3.   Roll the paper up with the cornstarch in it. Hand the rolled paper to the adult.

4.   Next, have the adult stand about three feet from the flame, take a breath, and blow the cornstarch out of the paper tube just above the flame. It will ignite and you'll see a large flame.

Very Important! The adult must breathe in *before* she puts the tube of cornstarch to her lips to avoid taking a gasp of cornstarch. This may seem like an idiotic piece of advice to you, but the second or third time I demonstrated this idea to a pile of kids I took just such a gasp. I placed the tube in my mouth and then took a deep breath. Bad idea. My eyes bugged out. I belched out a huge gasp of air, cornstarch went all over the classroom, and the kids were falling out of their chairs laughing while my eyes watered over to the point where I could not see and I was having severe pulmonary dysfunction.

Cornstarch Fireballs

5. If the adult is not quite successful the first time she tries this, ask her to do it again, aiming about a foot above the flame. Aiming higher allows the cornstarch to disperse, creating a larger surface area and a flame that is about four to six feet long. Guaranteed "ooh, aah."

How Come, Huh?

You have to have three things to make a fire—heat, oxygen, and fuel. In this case, the fuel was there, we had enough heat, and it was just the lack of enough exposure of surface area to oxygen that messed this up.

The cornstarch burst into flames when it was blown through the paper tube, and not when it was on the paper. When it was blown through the tube, there was a lot more surface area exposed to the oxygen. The more surface area that is exposed, the more opportunity there is for a chemical reaction, which in this case is combustion. If there is not enough oxygen, there won't be any fire.

Science Fair Extensions

22. You can run a hose into a closed metal tin, the kind that people give other people popcorn in at the holidays. Attach a funnel to the hose and fill the tin with cornstarch. Light a votive candle inside the tin, put the lid on, and blow into the hose. Grain Elevator Explosion!

Thanks and See You Soon!

That's it. Thanks for reading all the way through the book. We've been glad to share ideas with you, and we hope that you will try one of the other books in the series.

Science Fair Projects
•
A Step-by-Step Guide: From Idea to Presentation

Science Fair Projects

Ah, the impending science fair project—a good science fair project has the following five characteristics:

1. The student must come up with an *original* question.
2. That *original* question must be suited to an experiment in order to provide an answer.
3. The *original* idea is outlined with just one variable isolated.
4. The *original* experiment is performed and documented using the scientific method.
5. A presentation of the *original* idea in the form of a lab write-up and display board is completed.

Science Fair Projects

As simple as science fair projects versus science reports sounds, it gets screwed up millions of times a year by sweet, unsuspecting students who are counseled by sweet, unknowing, and probably just-as-confused parents.

To give you a sense of contrast, we have provided a list of legitimate science fair projects, as well as reports that do not qualify. We will also add some comments in italics that should help clarify why they do or do not qualify in the science fair project department.

Science Fair Projects

1. Temperature and the amount of time it takes mealworms to change to beetles.

Great start. We have chosen a single variable that is easy to measure: temperature. From this point forward the student can read, explore, and formulate an original question that is the foundation for the project.

A colleague of mine actually did a similar type of experiment for his master's degree. His topic: The rate of development of fly larvae in cow poop as a function of temperature. No kidding. He found out that the warmer the temperature of the poop, the faster the larvae developed into flies.

2. The effect of different concentrations of soapy water on seed germination.

Again, wonderful. Measuring the concentration of soapy water. This leads naturally into original questions and a good project.

3. Crystal size and the amount of sugar in the solution.

This could lead into other factors such as exploring the temperature of the solution, the size of the solution container, and other variables that may affect crystal growth. Opens a lot of doors.

vs. Science Reports

4.   Helicopter rotor size and the speed at which it falls.

Size also means surface area, which is very easy to measure. The student who did this not only found the mathematical threshold with relationship to air friction, but she had a ton of fun.

5.   The ideal ratio of baking soda to vinegar to make a fire extinguisher.

Another great start. Easy to measure and track, leads to a logical question that can either be supported or refuted with the data.

Each of these topics *measures* one thing, such as the amount of sugar, the concentration of soapy water, or the ideal size. If you start with an idea that allows you to measure something, then you can change it, ask questions, explore, and ultimately make a *prediction*, also called a *hypothesis*, and experiment to find out if you are correct. Here are some well-meaning but misguided entries:

Science Reports, <u>not Projects</u>
1. Dinosaurs!
OK, great. Everyone loves dinosaurs but where is the experiment? Did you find a new dinosaur? Is Jurassic Park alive and well, and we are headed there to breed, drug, or in some way test them? Probably not. This was a report on T. rex. Cool, but not a science fair project. And judging by the protest that this kid's mom put up when the kid didn't get his usual "A," it is a safe bet that she put a lot of time in and shared in the disappointment.

More Reports &

2. Our Friend the Sun

Another very large topic, no pun intended. This could be a great topic. Sunlight is fascinating. It can be split, polarized, reflected, refracted, measured, collected, converted. However, this poor kid simply chose to write about the size of the sun, regurgitate facts about its features, cycles, and other astrofacts while simultaneously offending the American Melanoma Survivors Society. Just kidding about that last part.

3. Smokers' Poll

A lot of folks think that they are headed in the right direction here. Again, it depends on how the kid attacks the idea. Are they going to single out race? Heredity? Shoe size? What exactly are they after here? The young lady who did this report chose to make it more of a psychology-studies effort than a scientific report. She wanted to know family income, if they fought with their parents, how much stress was on the job, and so on. All legitimate concerns but not placed in the right slot.

4. The Majestic Moose

If you went out and caught the moose, drugged it to see the side effects for disease control, or even mated it with an elk to determine if you could create an animal that would become the spokesanimal for the Alabama Dairy Farmers' Got Melk? promotion, that would be fine. But, another fact-filled report should be filed with the English teacher.

5. How Tadpoles Change into Frogs

Great start, but they forgot to finish the statement. We know how tadpoles change into frogs. What we don't know is how tadpoles change into frogs if they are in an altered environment, if they are hatched out of cycle, if they are stuck under the tire of an off-road vehicle blatantly driving through a protected wetland area. That's what we want to know. How tadpoles change into frogs, if, when, or under what measurable circumstances.

Now that we have beaten the chicken squat out of this introduction, we are going to show you how to pick a topic that can be adapted to become a successful science fair project after one more thought.

One Final Comment

A Gentle Reminder

Quite often I discuss the scientific method with moms and dads, teachers and kids, and get the impression that, according to their understanding, there is one, and only one, scientific method. This is not necessarily true. There are lots of ways to investigate the world we live in and on.

Paleontologists dig up dead animals and plants but have no way to conduct experiments on them. They're dead. Albert Einstein, the most famous scientist of the last century and probably on everybody's starting five of all time, never did experiments. He was a theoretical physicist, which means that he came up with a hypothesis, skipped over collecting materials for things like black holes and space-time continuums, didn't experiment on anything or even collect data. He just went straight from hypothesis to conclusion, and he's still considered part of the scientific community. You'll probably follow the six steps we outline, but keep an open mind.

Project Planner

This outline is designed to give you a specific set of timelines to follow as you develop your science fair project. Most teachers will give you 8 to 11 weeks notice for this kind of assignment. We are going to operate from the shorter timeline with our suggested schedule, which means that the first thing you need to do is get a calendar.

A. The suggested time to be devoted to each item is listed in parentheses next to that item. Enter the date of the Science Fair and then, using the calendar, work backward, entering dates.

B. As you complete each item, enter the date that you completed it in the column between the goal (due date) and project item.

Goal   *Completed*   *Project Item*

1. Generate a Hypothesis (2 weeks)

_____	_____	Review Idea Section, pp. 158–159
_____	_____	Try Several Experiments
_____	_____	Hypothesis Generated
_____	_____	Finished Hypothesis Submitted
_____	_____	Hypothesis Approved

2. Gather Background Information (1 week)

_____	_____	Concepts/Discoveries Written Up
_____	_____	Vocabulary/Glossary Completed
_____	_____	Famous Scientists in Field

& Timeline

Goal Completed Project Item

3. Design an Experiment (1 week)

____	____	Procedure Written
____	____	Lab Safety Review Completed
____	____	Procedure Approved
____	____	Data Tables Prepared
____	____	Materials List Completed
____	____	Materials Acquired

4. Perform the Experiment (2 weeks)

____	____	Scheduled Lab Time

5. Collect and Record Experimental Data (part of 4)

____	____	Data Tables Completed
____	____	Graphs Completed
____	____	Other Data Collected and Prepared

6. Present Your Findings (2 weeks)

____	____	Rough Draft of Paper Completed
____	____	Proofreading Completed
____	____	Final Report Completed
____	____	Display Completed
____	____	Oral Report Outlined on Index Cards
____	____	Practice Presentation of Oral Report
____	____	Oral Report Presentation
____	____	Science Fair Setup
____	____	Show Time!

Scientific Method
• Step 1 •
The Hypothesis

The Hypothesis

A hypothesis is an educated guess. It is a statement of what you think will probably happen. It is also the most important part of your science fair project because it directs the entire process. It determines what you study, the materials you will need, and how the experiment will be designed, carried out, and evaluated. Needless to say, you need to put some thought into this part.

There are four steps to generating a hypothesis:

Step One • Pick a Topic
Preferably something that you are interested in studying. We would like to politely recommend that you take a peek at physical science ideas (physics and chemistry) if you are a rookie and this is one of your first shots at a science fair project. These kinds of lab ideas allow you to repeat experiments quickly. There is a lot of data that can be collected, and there is a huge variety to choose from.

If you are having trouble finding an idea, all you have to do is pick up a compilation of science activities (like this one) and start thumbing through it. Go to the local library or head to a bookstore and you will find a wide and ever-changing selection to choose from. Find a topic that interests you and start reading. At some point, an idea will catch your eye, and you will be off to the races.

Pick an Idea You Like

We hope you find an idea you like between the covers of this book. But we also realize that 1) there are more ideas than we have included in this book, and 2) other kinds of presentations, or methods of writing labs, may be just what you need to trigger a new idea or put a different spin on things. So, without further ado, we introduce you to several additional titles that may be of help to you in developing a science fair project.

1. Simple Chemistry Experiments with Everyday Materials. Written by Louis V. Loesching. ISBN 0-8069-0688-x. Published by Sterling. 128 pages.

One hundred and ten experiments, all using common household items. This book covers crystals, solutions, matter, and a host of other topics, including some fun puzzles at the end where you become a science detective and solve some mysteries. Great book for extending the ideas from *Le Boom du Jour.*

2. Chemistry for Every Kid. Written by Janice Van Cleave. ISBN 0-471-62085-8. Published by John Wiley & Sons. 232 pages.

Part of her very popular *Science for Every Kid* series, this book has 101 hands-on science activities that cover a very broad range of experiments, some of which could double as electricity, fluid dynamics, thermodynamics, or mechanics experiments. Chapter topics include matter, pH, gases, phase changes, solutions, heat, and acids and bases.

The experiments are all very simple, generally use easy-to-find household materials, and come with entertaining illustrations. Weak in the extension department, but you should have a handle on that after reading this book anyway.

3. Cool Chemistry. Great Experiments with Simple Stuff. Written by Steve W. Moje. ISBN 0-8069-6349-2. Published by Sterling. 96 pages.

This book has 56 cool chemistry experiments. The instructions are very clear and the illustrations help the reader get through the main ideas easily. Topics include physical properties of matter, mixtures and solutions, acids and bases, and food chemistry. It's a great place to pick up where *Chemhead* left off. Plenty of new ideas.

4. Chemistry Basics. Written by Penny Raife Durant. ISBN 0-531-10971-2. Published by Franklin Watts. 32 pages.

If you have a younger student who really enjoyed the very basic ideas in this book, then Penny's book is for you. It has 12 simple experiments that reinforce ideas covered in *Jr. Chemhead*. You will explore absorption and repulsion of water, density, solubility, and changes of state, and you'll experiment with a little bit of chromatography. This book has the best illustrations of the six reviewed on these pages.

5. Experiments with Bubbles. Written by Robert Gardner. ISBN 0-89490-666-6. Published by Enslow. 104 pages.

If you got a big kick out of the last section of this book and really want to delve into the science of bubbleology, then this is a great book. Gardner takes you through 36 different bubble-related experiments, ranging from the chemistry of bubbles, to their geometry, design, properties of light, and tensile strength. You will be a bubblexpert when you are done with this book.

6. Science Projects about Kitchen Chemistry. Written by Robert Gardner. ISBN 0-89490-953-3. Published by Enslow. 128 pages.

Robert Gardner is a very well-known science educator who has written a wheelbarrow full of hands-on science books. This particular work contains 45 experiments that investigate the three major food groups, liquids, acids and bases, and a host of other ideas.

Develop an Original Idea

Step Two • Do the Lab

Choose a lab activity that looks interesting and try the experiment. Some kids make the mistake of thinking that all you have to do is find a lab in a book, repeat the lab, and you are on the gravy train with biscuit wheels. Your goal is to ask an ORIGINAL question, not repeat an experiment that has been done a bazillion times before.

As you do the lab, be thinking not only about the data you are collecting, but of ways you could adapt or change the experiment to find out new information. The point of the science fair project is to have you become an actual scientist and contribute a little bit of new knowledge to the world.

You know that they don't pay all of those engineers good money to sit around and repeat other people's lab work. The company wants new ideas, so if you are able to generate and explore new ideas, you become very valuable, not only to that company but to society. It is the question-askers who find cures for diseases, create new materials, figure out ways to make existing machines energy efficient, and change the way that we live. For the purpose of illustration, we are going to take a lab titled, "Prisms, Water Prisms," from another book, *Photon U*, and run it through the rest of the process. The lab uses a tub of water, an ordinary mirror, and light to create a prism that splits the light into the spectrum of the rainbow. Cool. Easy to do. Not expensive and open to all kinds of adaptations, including the four that we discuss on the next page.

Step Three • *Bend, Fold, Spindle, & Mutilate Your Lab*

Once you have picked out an experiment, ask if it is possible to do any of the following things to modify it into an original experiment. You want to try to change the experiment to make it more interesting and find out one new, small piece of information.

Heat it	Freeze it	Reverse it	Double it
Bend it	Invert it	Poison it	Dehydrate it
Drown it	Stretch it	Fold it	Ignite it
Split it	Irradiate it	Oxidize it	Reduce it
Chill it	Speed it up	Color it	Grease it
Expand it	Substitute it	Remove it	Slow it down

If you take a look at our examples, that's exactly what we did to the main idea. We took the list of 24 different things that you could do to an experiment—not nearly all of them, by the way—and tried a couple of them out on the prism setup.

Double it: Get a second prism and see if you can continue to separate the colors farther by lining up a second prism in the rainbow of the first.

Reduce it: Figure out a way to gather up the colors that have been produced and mix them back together to produce white light again.

Reverse it: Experiment with moving the flashlight and paper closer to the mirror and farther away. Draw a picture and be able to predict what happens to the size and clarity of the rainbow image.

Substitute it: You can also create a rainbow on a sunny day using a garden hose with a fine-spray nozzle attached. Set the nozzle adjustment so that a fine mist is produced and move the mist around in the sunshine until you see the rainbow. This works better if the sun is lower in the sky; late afternoon is best.

Hypothesis Worksheet

Step Three (Expanded) • *Bend, Fold, Spindle Worksheet*
This worksheet will give you an opportunity to work through the process of creating an original idea.

A. Write down the lab idea that you want to mangle.

_____

_____

_____

_____

B. List the possible variables you could change in the lab.

   i. _____

   ii. _____

   iii. _____

   iv. _____

   v. _____

C. Take one variable listed in section B and apply one of the 24 changes listed below to it. Write that change down and state your new lab idea in the space below. Do that with three more changes.

Heat it	Freeze it	Reverse it	Double it
Bend it	Invert it	Poison it	Dehydrate it
Drown it	Stretch it	Fold it	Ignite it
Split it	Irradiate it	Oxidize it	Reduce it
Chill it	Speed it up	Color it	Grease it
Expand it	Substitute it	Remove it	Slow it down

   i. _____

_____

_____

_____

Le Boom du Jour • *B. K. Hixson*

ii. _____

_____

_____

_____

iii. _____

_____

_____

_____

iv. _____

STRETCHING!

_____

_____

_____

Step Four • Create an Original Idea—Your Hypothesis
Your hypothesis should be stated as an opinion. You've done the basic experiment, you've made observations, you're not stupid. Put two and two together and make a PREDICTION. Be sure that you are experimenting with just a single variable.

State your hypothesis in the space below. List the variable.

A. _____

_____

_____

_____

B. Variable tested: _____

Sample Hypothesis Worksheet

On the previous two pages is a worksheet that will help you develop your thoughts and a hypothesis. Here is sample of the finished product to help you understand how to use it.

A. Write down the lab idea that you want to mutilate.

A mirror is placed in a tub of water. A beam of light is focused through the water onto the mirror, producing a rainbow on the wall.

B. List the possible variables you could change in the lab.
    i. **Source of light**
    ii. **The liquid in the tub**
    iii. **The distance from flashlight to mirror**

C. Take one variable listed in section B and apply one of the 24 changes to it. Write that change down and state your new lab idea in the space below.

The shape of the beam of light can be controlled by making and placing cardboard filters over the end of the flashlight. Various shapes such as circles, squares, and slits will produce different quality rainbows.

D. State your hypothesis in the space below. List the variable. Be sure that when you write the hypothesis you are stating an idea and <u>not asking a question.</u>

Hypothesis: The narrower the beam of light, the tighter, brighter, and more focused the reflected rainbow will appear.

Variable tested: **the opening on the filter**

Scientific Method
• Step 2 •
Gather Information

Gather Information

Read about your topic and find out what we already know. Check books, videos, the Internet, and movies, talk with experts in the field, and molest an encyclopedia or two. Gather as much information as you can before you begin planning your experiment.

In particular, there are several things that you will want to pay special attention to and that should accompany any good science fair project.

A. Major Scientific Concepts

Be sure that you research and explain the main idea(s) that is / are driving your experiment. It may be a law of physics or chemical rule or an explanation of an aspect of plant physiology.

B. Scientific Words

As you use scientific terms in your paper, you should also define them in the margins of the paper or in a glossary at the end of the report. You cannot assume that everyone knows about geothermal energy transmutation in sulfur-loving bacterium. Be prepared to define some new terms for them. . . and scrub your hands really well when you are done if that is your project.

C. Historical Perspective

When did we first learn about this idea, and who is responsible for getting us this far? You need to give a historical perspective with names, dates, countries, awards, and other recognition.

Building a Research Foundation

1. This sheet is designed to help you organize your thoughts and give you some ideas on where to look for information on your topic. When you prepare your lab report, you will want to include the background information outlined below.

A. *Major Scientific Concepts (Two is plenty.)*

i. _____

_____

_____

_____

ii. _____

_____

_____

_____

B. *Scientific Words (No more than 10)*

i. _____

ii. _____

iii. _____

iv. _____

v. _____

vi. _____

vii. _____

viii. _____

ix. _____

x. _____

C. *Historical Perspective*
Add this as you find it.

2. There are several sources of information that are available to help you fill in the details from the previous page.

A. *Contemporary Print Resources*
   (Magazines, Newspapers, Journals)

   i. _____
   ii. _____
   iii. _____
   iv. _____
   v. _____
   vi. _____

B. *Other Print Resources*
   (Books, Encyclopedias, Dictionaries, Textbooks)

   i. _____
   ii. _____
   iii. _____
   iv. _____
   v. _____
   vi. _____

C. *Celluloid Resources*
   (Films, Filmstrips, Videos)

   i. _____
   ii. _____
   iii. _____
   iv. _____
   v. _____
   vi. _____

D. Electronic Resources
   (Internet Website Addresses, DVDs, MP3s)

    i. _____

    ii. _____

    iii. _____

    iv. _____

    v. _____

    vi. _____

    vii. _____

    viii. _____

    ix. _____

    x. _____

E. Human Resources
   (Scientists, Engineers, Professionals, Professors, Teachers)

    i. _____

    ii. _____

    iii. _____

    iv. _____

    v. _____

    vi. _____

You may want to keep a record of all of your research and add it to the back of the report as an Appendix. Some teachers who are into volume think this is really cool. Others, like myself, find it a pain in the tuchus. No matter what you do, be sure to keep an accurate record of where you find data. If you quote from a report word for word, be sure to give proper credit with either a footnote or parenthetical reference. This is very important for credibility and accuracy. This is will keep you out of trouble with plagiarism (copying without giving credit).

Scientific Method
• Step 3 •
Design Your Experiment

Le Boom du Jour • *B. K. Hixson*

Acquire Your Lab Materials

The purpose of this section is to help you plan your experiment. You'll make a map of where you are going, how you want to get there, and what you will take along.

List the materials you will need to complete your experiment in the table below. Be sure to list multiples if you will need more than one item. Many science materials double as household items in their spare time. Check around the house before you buy anything from a science supply company or hardware store. For your convenience, we have listed some suppliers on page 19 of this book.

Material	Qty.	Source	$
1.			
2.			
3.			
4.			
5.			
6.			
7.			
8.			
9.			
10.			
11.			
12.			

Total $_____

Outline Your Experiment

This sheet is designed to help you outline your experiment. If you need more space, make a copy of this page to finish your outline. When you are done with this sheet, review it with an adult, make any necessary changes, review safety concerns on the next page, prepare your data tables, gather your equipment, and start to experiment.

In the space below, list what you are going to do in the order you are going to do it.

i. _____

_____

_____

_____

ii. _____

_____

_____

_____

iii. _____

_____

_____

_____

iv. _____

_____

_____

_____

v. _____

_____

_____

_____

Evaluate Safety Concerns

We have included an overall safety section in the front of this book on pages 16–18, but there are some very specific questions you need to ask, and prepare for, depending on the needs of your experiment. If you find that you need to prepare for any of these safety concerns, place a check mark next to the letter.

_____ *A. Goggles & Eyewash Station*
If you are mixing chemicals or working with materials that might splinter or produce flying objects, goggles and an eyewash station or sink with running water should be available.

_____ *B. Ventilation*
If you are mixing chemicals that could produce fire, smoke, fumes, or obnoxious odors, you will need to use a vented hood or go outside and perform the experiment in the fresh air.

_____ *C. Fire Blanket or Fire Extinguisher*
If you are working with potentially combustible chemicals or electricity, a fire blanket and extinguisher nearby are a must.

_____ *D. Chemical Disposal*
If your experiment produces a poisonous chemical or there are chemical-filled tissues (as in dissected animals), you may need to make arrangements to dispose of the by-products from your lab.

_____ *E. Electricity*
If you are working with materials and developing an idea that uses electricity, make sure that the wires are in good repair, that the electrical demand does not exceed the capacity of the supply, and that your work area is grounded.

_____ *F. Emergency Phone Numbers*
Look up and record the following phone numbers for the Fire Department: _____ , Poison Control: _____ , and Hospital: _____ . Post them in an easy-to-find location.

Prepare Data Tables

Finally, you will want to prepare your data tables and have them ready to go before you start your experiment. Each data table should be easy to understand and easy for you to use.

A good data table has a **title** that describes the information being collected, and it identifies the **variable** and the **unit** being collected on each data line. The variable is *what* you are measuring and the unit is *how* you are measuring it. Variables are usually written like this:

Variable (unit), or to give you some examples:

Time (seconds)
Distance (meters)
Electricity (volts)

An example of a well-prepared data table looks like the sample below. We've cut the data table into thirds because the book is too small to display the whole line.

Determining the Boiling Point of Compound X_1

Time (min.)	0	1	2	3	4	5	6
Temp. ($^{\circ}$C)							

Time (min.)	7	8	9	10	11	12	13
Temp. ($^{\circ}$C)							

Time (min.)	14	15	16	17	18	19	20
Temp. ($^{\circ}$C)							

Scientific Method
• Step 4 •
Conduct the Experiment

Lab Time

It's time to get going. You've generated a hypothesis, collected the materials, written out the procedure, checked the safety issues, and prepared your data tables. Fire it up. Here's the short list of things to remember as you experiment.

_____ *A. Follow the Procedure, Record Any Changes*

Follow your own directions specifically as you wrote them. If you find the need to change the procedure once you are into the experiment, that's fine; it's part of the process. Make sure to keep detailed records of the changes. When you repeat the experiment a second or third time, follow the new directions exactly.

_____ *B. Observe Safety Rules*

It's easier to complete the lab activity if you are in the lab rather than the emergency room.

_____ *C. Record Data Immediately*

Collect temperatures, distances, voltages, revolutions, and any other variables and immediately record them into your data table. Do not think you will be able to remember them and fill everything in after the lab is completed.

_____ *D. Repeat the Experiment Several Times*

The more data that you collect, the better. It will give you a larger data base and your averages will be more meaningful. As you do multiple experiments, be sure to identify each data set by date and time so you can separate them out.

_____ *E. Prepare for Extended Experiments*

Some experiments require days or weeks to complete, particularly those with plants and animals or the growing of crystals. Prepare a safe place for your materials so your experiment can continue undisturbed while you collect the data. Be sure you've allowed enough time for your due date.

Scientific Method
• Step 5 •
Collect and Display Data

Types of Graphs

This section will give you some ideas on how you can display the information you are going to collect as a graph. A graph is simply a picture of the data that you gathered portrayed in a manner that is quick and easy to reference. There are four kinds of graphs described on the next two pages. If you find you need a leg up in the graphing department, we have a book in the series called *Data Tables & Graphing*. It will guide you through the process.

Line and Bar Graphs

These are the most common kinds of graphs. The most consistent variable is plotted on the "x," or horizontal, axis and the more temperamental variable is plotted along the "y," or vertical, axis. Each data point on a line graph is recorded as a dot on the graph and then all of the dots are connected to form a picture of the data. A bar graph starts on the horizontal axis and moves up to the data line.

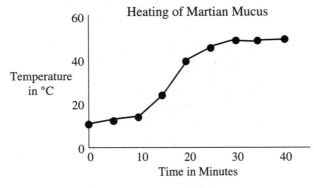

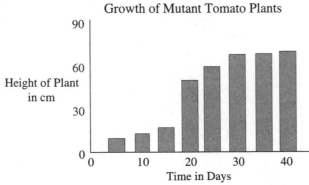

Best Fit Graphs

A best fit graph was created to show averages or trends rather than specific data points. The data that has been collected is plotted on a graph just as on a line graph, but instead of drawing a line from point to point to point, which sometimes is impossible anyway, you just freehand a line that hits "most of the data."

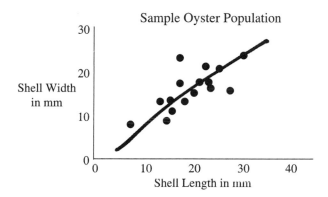

Pie Graphs

Pie graphs are used to show relationships between different groups. All of the data is totaled up and a percentage is determined for each group. The pie is then divided to show the relationship between one group and another.

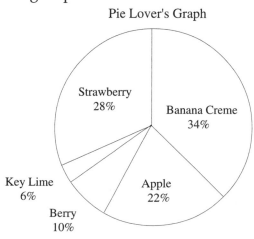

Other Kinds of Data

1. Written Notes & Observations

This is the age-old technique used by all scientists. Record your observations in a lab book. Written notes can be made quickly as the experiment is proceeding, and they can then be expounded upon later. Quite often notes made in the heat of an experiment are revisited during the evaluation portion of the process, and they can shed valuable light on how or why the experiment went the way it did.

2. Drawings

Quick sketches as well as fully developed drawings can be used as a way to report data for a science experiment. Be sure to title each drawing and, if possible, label what it is that you are looking at. Drawings that are actual size are best.

3. Photographs, Videotapes, and Audiotapes

Usually better than drawings, quicker, and more accurate, but you do have the added expense and time of developing the film. However, they can often capture images and details that are not usually seen by the naked eye.

4. The Experiment Itself

Some of the best data you can collect and present is the actual experiment itself. Nothing will speak more effectively for you than the plants you grew, the specimens you collected, or that big pile of tissue that was an armadillo you peeled from the tread of an 18-wheeler.

Scientific Method
• Step 6 •
Present Your Ideas

Oral Report Checklist

It is entirely possible that you will be asked to make an oral presentation to your classmates. This will give you an opportunity to explain what you did and how you did it. Quite often this presentation is part of your overall score, so if you do well, it will enhance your chances for one of the bigger awards.

To prepare for your oral report, your science fair presentation should include the following components:

Physical Display

_____a.   freestanding display board
                hypothesis
                data tables, graphs, photos, etc.
                abstract (short summary)

_____b.   actual lab setup (equipment)

Oral Report

_____a.   hypothesis or question
_____b.   background information
                concepts
                word definitions
                history or scientists
_____c.   experimental procedure
_____d.   data collected
                data tables
                graphs
                photos or drawings
_____e.   conclusions and findings
_____f.   ask for questions

Set the display board up next to you on the table. Transfer the essential information to index cards. Use the index cards for reference, but do not read from them. Speak in a clear voice, hold your head up, and make eye contact with your peers. Ask if there are any questions before you finish and sit down.

Written Report Checklist

Next up is the written report, also called your lab write-up. After you compile or sort the data you have collected during the experiment and evaluate the results, you will be able to come to a conclusion about your hypothesis. Remember, disproving an idea is as valuable as proving it.

This sheet is designed to help you write up your science fair project and present your data in an organized manner. This is a final checklist for you.

To prepare your write-up, your science fair report should include the following components:

_____	a.	binder
_____	b.	cover page, title, & your name
_____	c.	abstract (one paragraph summary)
_____	d.	table of contents with page numbers
_____	e.	hypothesis or question
_____	f.	background information
		concepts
		word definitions
		history or scientists
_____	g.	list of materials used
_____	h.	experimental procedure
		written description
		photo or drawing of setup
_____	i.	data collected
		data tables
		graphs
		photos or drawings
_____	j.	conclusions and findings
_____	k.	glossary of terms
_____	l.	references

Display Checklist

Prepare your display to accompany the report. A good display should include the following:

Freestanding Display

_____ a.   freestanding cardboard back
_____ b.   title of experiment
_____ c.   your name
_____ d.   hypothesis
_____ e.   findings of the experiment
_____ f.   photos or illustrations of equipment
_____ g.   data tables or graphs

Additional Display Items

_____ h.   a copy of the write-up
_____ i.   actual lab equipment setup

Glossary, Index, and More Ideas

Glossary

Acid
Any compound that has a pH below 7.0. Acids have lots of free hydrogen atoms to react with other compounds. Some common examples of acids are found in oranges, grapefruits, lemons, tangerines, and strawberries.

Atom
The smallest complete building block of the universe. These are also elements, and as of this writing, there were just over 100 of them. Some of the more famous are oxygen, carbon, hydrogen, gold, lead, copper, helium, iron, calcium, and einsteinium.

Bipolar Molecule
A molecule with a strange mental disorder... nope, check that. A fixed arrangement of atoms. If one end of the molecule exhibits a positive charge and the other end exhibits a negative charge, it is said to be bipolar or have two poles. The molecules are like little magnets and are very important in transferring other atoms through wall membranes, cell walls, and other biochemical check points.

Boiling Point
The temperature at which a compound changes from a liquid to a gas. Fixed for each and every compound, this is an identifying trait that allows chemists to identify and separate compounds.

Buoyant Force
The upward pressure exerted by a liquid on an object floating in that liquid—a function, in part, of the density of that liquid.

Change of State
The term, "state," refers to solids, liquids, and gases. When a liquid changes from a solid to a liquid or a liquid to a solid, when a liquid changes to a gas or a gas to a liquid, or if a solid changes to a gas, it is called a change of state. No relocation necessary.

Glossary

Chemical Change

Two or more chemicals combining to form a new compound with new characteristics. Indicators of this are a change in state, color, temperature, density, odor, or magnetism. This new compound also has a new boiling point, melting point, density, and so on. It's a complete makeover from a molecular point of view.

Chemical Formulas

A combination of letters and numbers representing molecules and atoms, written as an equation showing the changes and new by-products. Shorthand for chemists.

Chromotography

The separation of colors, pigments, or molecules in general, by using a solvent and a porous piece of paper or a gel and an electrical charge. The compound separates from lightest to heaviest or by charges.

Cohesion

Attraction between two bipolar molecules. Generally not something that we discuss in front of the kids.

Colloid

A solid, liquid, or gas that is dispersed into a second solid, liquid, or gas but is not chemically connected to that other compound. Styrofoam is one of the more famous examples. Air is trapped in spaces created when polystyrene plastic is extracted from a mold. The air is still air, and the polystyrene is still polystyrene. They just happen to like to hang out together.

Convection Current

The movement of hot air or water in an upward motion relative to the cooler surrounding air or liquid. Warm liquids or gases rise and cool ones sink. This sinking and rising creates a current.

Glossary

Crystallization
The slow cooling or evaporation of a liquid that allows for the orderly deposition of atoms and molecules to form solid crystals. The slower the process, the bigger the crystals are.

Density
Mass divided by volume. This number tells you how tightly packed the atoms in your sample are compared with other samples.

Effervescence
Gas displaced in a liquid by a solid. When this happens, the gas can leave in a big hurry and produce a tremendous amount of foam.

Elements
Atoms. The Periodic Table of the Elements is the Yellow Pages™ of the atom community and provides information about structure, reactivity, state, and mass, among other things.

Emulsion
Two liquids that have been mixed together and remain mixed but do not react with one another chemically. Mayonnaise is an excellent example of an emulsion of egg yolks and oil. They have been beaten together but have not reacted with each other to form a brand new compound.

Endothermic
A chemical reaction that absorbs heat from the environment. It feels cool to the touch.

Evaporation
A change in state from liquid to gas.

Exothermic
A chemical reaction that releases heat into the environment. It feels warm or hot to the touch.

Glossary

Filtering

A method of separating mixtures by pouring them through a porous piece of paper called a filter. Once in the paper, the liquids pass through and the solids remain on the surface. Coffee anyone?

Freezing Point

The temperature at which a free-flowing liquid changes to a solid compound. For deer, it is the minute that the car turns the bend and the headlights illuminate them. Fixed for each and every compound, this is an identifying trait that allows chemists to identify and separate compounds. Cousin to the melting point.

Graph

Quick, easy-to-view picture of data. There are several kinds of graphs: pie, bar, line, best fit, and pictorial.

Hydrophilic

A molecule or compound that is absorbed by or is solvent in water. *Water-loving* is the literal translation from the Latin.

Hydrophobic

A molecule or compound that is repelled by water. *Water-fearing* is the literal translation from the Latin.

Insolubility

A compound, solid, liquid, or gas that will not dissolve into another liquid or gas. They do not play well with one another.

Melting Point

A fixed, characteristic temperature at which a compound changes from a solid to a liquid. Fixed for each and every compound, this is an identifying trait that allows chemists to identify and separate compounds. Cousin to the freezing point.

Glossary

Meniscus
A dip or downward bow in the level of the water held in a narrow cylinder. The bottom level of the meniscus is an accurate reflection of the amount of water in the container.

Physical Change
Tearing, ripping, folding, stomping, squashing, or any other random mutilation exacted on a compound that does not change its chemical nature or inherent characteristics.

Solvent
A liquid or gas that allows a second, different compound to disperse or dissolve in between its molecules.

Sublimation
A relatively unusual compound that changes directly from a gas to a solid or a solid to gas without taking time to pass through the liquid state. Dry ice is a great example of this.

Suspension
Solid particles evenly mixed into and floating around in a liquid. Milk is a suspension of protein and fat in liquid.

Thermometer
A tool that measures the average amount of heat in a substance.

Index

Index

Index

Notes

Notes

Notes

Notes

Notes

Notes

Notes

Notes

Notes

Notes

Notes

Notes

Notes

Notes

More Science Books

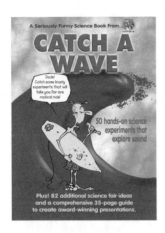

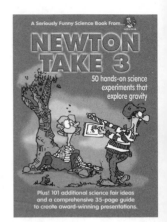

Catch a Wave
50 hands-on lab activities that sound off on the topic of noise, vibration, waves, the Doppler effect, and associated ideas.

Thermodynamic Thrills
50 hands-on lab activities that investigate heat via conduction, convection, radiation, specific heat, and temperature.

Newton Take 3
50 hands-on lab activities that explore the world of mechanics, forces, gravity, and Newton's three laws of motion.

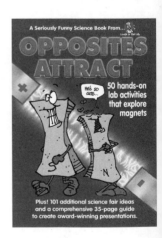

Gravity Works
50 hands-on lab activities from the world of things that fly. Air, air pressure, Bernoulli's law, and all things that fly, float, or glide are explored.

Electron Herding 101
50 hands-on lab activities that introduce static electricity, circuit electricity, and include a number of fun and very easy-to-build projects.

Opposites Attract
50 hands-on lab activities that delve into the world of natural and man-made magnets as well as the characteristics of magnetic attraction.

Le Boom du Jour • B. K. Hixson